# ENDORSEMENTS AND COMMENTS

## *This Book Raised Me*

As a young woman in the early seventies, I found myself a wife and a mother without skills to do either very well. What did God expect of me in training my children? How could I teach them, since I was an inexperienced Christian myself? Where could I find instruction for a better marriage? How could I fit my already busy life into God's service?

Then I found Jane McWhorter's book, *She Hath Done What She Could*. This book answered so many of my questions! Before she ever met me, Jane was 'raising' this young wife and mother to do it God's way!

Jane McWhorter took seriously the command in Titus 2:3–5 to teach the younger women how to "love their husbands and to love their children." Jane has helped me so many times through her books. And I went to *She Hath Done What She Could* over and over until it was dog-eared.

Not everyone had Christian influences as they were growing up. I was one who struggled with my Christianity in my youth. I looked to experienced Christian role models for guidance.

Jane was my mentor without even realizing it. I have always loved her and appreciated all her guidance even though I met her only at lectureships and ladies' days. She was an outstanding Christian lady who left a legacy so that even today she is "raising" a new generation, not to mention her inspiration in all of her writings to those of us now in our more mature years! She motivates us to continue in His Word through her writings.

I wholeheartedly endorse *She Hath Done What She Could* in its facelifted revision—it is a faith lift as well. I look forward to studying it with my ladies' class.

—Teresa Glenn
Lynchburg, Virginia

## *Mom's First Book*

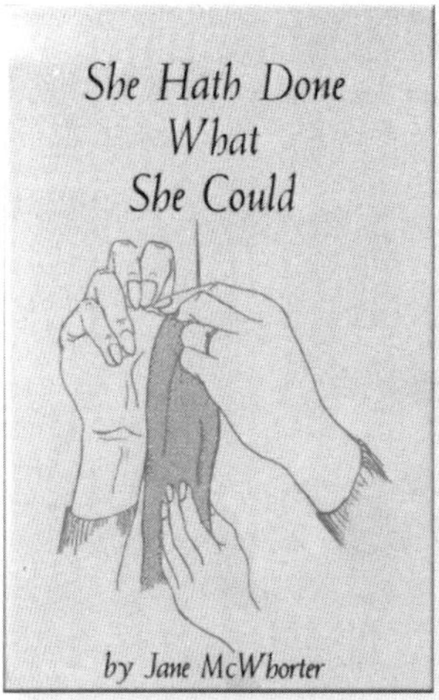


Back in the sixties, Mom's days were filled with raising children, teaching school, and being a preacher's wife. She tossed around ideas for a book she would write someday.

Little did she imagine the future! Following a car accident that nearly cost her life, Mom's recovery period provided her a lot of time to think. She realized that each day was a precious gift and that "someday" was not guaranteed. When she was strong enough to sit up, Mom began the painstaking task of typing her thoughts. It was a laborious process, accomplished by the use of a manual typewriter and a single finger, which was her only functioning one.

She presented me with my own copy of the original *She Hath Done What She Could* on my nineteenth birthday. The dedication page read "Lovingly dedicated to use in His service from a heart overflowing with love and gratitude for the gift of life itself." Mom added, "And for the special privilege of being allowed to see you reach your adult years!"

This book ignited a passion for writing in Mom. Nothing would please her more than to know that her work is continuing, even though she has gone on to be with the Lord. I am gratefully reminded of Hebrews 11:4—(s)he being dead still speaks.

—Kathy McWhorter Kendall

## *Mom Did What She Could*

As news traveled regarding Mom's condition, close to a thousand letters flooded the hospital. Mom confided, "I don't understand why so many people are writing me letters. I've never done anything special; I simply do what everyone else does!"

I replied, "Well, Mom, you have written over a dozen books and have groups who fly you all over the United States to speak at their conferences." But she just shook her head.

As Mom dozed, I began to read the letters. As touched as I was with what people said, the greater impact lay in what they did not say. The majority never mentioned anything about Mom's books or her speaking engagements. Instead, letter after letter shared how she had shown them some act of kindness, some dating back thirty or more years:

- You wrote me notes of encouragement.
- You always remembered birthdays and anniversaries.
- You shared a cup of coffee and a listening ear when problems overwhelmed me.
- You regularly visited my mom at the nursing home.
- You came by to encourage me in jail.
- You dropped by my house simply to give me a hug and a single rose after my miscarriage when I was a single girl.

Nothing Mom did was expensive, out of the ordinary, or time consuming. She was loved because she didn't wait on the monumental opportunity for a good deed. Instead she acted on the daily, seemingly insignificant opportunities to ease a burden and show an act of kindness. Don't we often walk right past the same opportunities and either ignore them or choose no action?

When Mom awakened, I told her about reading the letters. "I know now what you meant when you said you'd never done anything out of the ordinary."

Mom smiled, nodded, and said, "You get it." She wanted me to know that a life of tremendous impact isn't dependent on being a bestselling author or a speaker. Instead, we make deep impressions when we act on the small, seemingly insignificant opportunities to extend the love of God.

Her life was well spent. Simply put . . . Mom did what she could.

—Greg McWhorter

# She Hath Done What She Could

Jane McWhorter

Publishing Designs, Inc.
P.O. Box 3241
Huntsville, Alabama 35810

Publishing Designs, Inc.
P.O. Box 3241
Huntsville, Alabama 35810





Page design and layout: Crosslin Creative

Images: dollarphotoclub.com, vectorstock.com

Editor: Peggy Coulter



Printed in the United States of America.

---

Publisher's Cataloging-in-Publication Data

McWhorter, Jane, 1935–2013

She Hath Done What She Could / Jane McWhorter

1. Christian Women—Opportunities. 2. Christian Women—Roles and Duties.

I. McWhorter, Jane II. Title

ISBN 978-0-929540-91-7

248.8

Lovingly dedicated to use in His service
from a heart overflowing with love
and gratitude for the gift of life itself.

# TABLE OF CONTENTS

# PREFACE

## *What Is That in Thine Hand?*

These lessons come from a heart overflowing with love and gratitude to Almighty God. I completed the rough manuscript before my husband, children, and I were involved in a head-on collision in October 1970. When the cast was removed from my right hand—one of my many injuries—I had no use of that hand. Three different nerves were injured. The doctors gave me little real hope of ever using it again.

During the months that followed, I thought a lot about hands as mine lay in two different braces. I promised God that I would not complain over the loss of the use of any of my limbs. It seemed that my mind and the rest of my body were going to be normal, and I was very grateful for that.

As I looked at my hands, I thought back over the years. I confess I took them for granted then. Slowly, after much exercise, the injured hand gradually became more functional. How well I remember the time I was able to pat my little boy's sleeping face. How strange. I had never even considered that as a blessing.

The creeping recovery continued. I had to write and type with my left hand. Every day I gave myself "writing lessons." Slowly, reluctantly, those torn-up muscles began to obey my brain.

Now, although my little finger will not bend, I use my right hand quite normally—cooking, washing, sweeping, sewing for my daughter. I have even returned to the task of teaching third graders how to write. (I now teach with more sympathy and understanding.) Wouldn't your heart overflow with thanksgiving for such blessings?

The personal references serve one purpose. I am saying to you: *Don't take the ability to use your hands for granted.*

We may not possess any special talent, but no extraordinary abilities are required for the services discussed in this book—only a desire to try. Remember, the one-talent man was not condemned for not possessing several talents. He was rebuked for hiding that talent—for not even trying to use it to serve his master (Matthew 25:24–27).

Take a good look at your hands. If they are reasonably normal, put them to work in God's service. Examine the common things within your grasp—a pen, a coffee pot, a covered dish, a Bible, a Bible storybook, flannel graph figures, a wedding ring, a broom and mop, a scrap of material, a tin can, a child's tiny fingers, scissors, a paintbrush, a steering wheel, a flower pot, a tract, a DVD—all everyday objects that any woman can use to glorify God. The anointing of Christ's feet required no special ability—only a precious ointment and willing hands. Our Lord rewarded this menial task with the promise: "Wherever this gospel is preached in the whole world, what this woman has done will also be told as a memorial to her" (Mark 14:9). *She hath done what she could.* She used what was in her hands.

Think of Christ's hands. The same hands that touched little children and healed the sick also knew agony and suffering as they were nailed to the cross.

- Those scarred hands were instrumental in proving the divinity of our Lord to His apostles: "Behold My hands and My feet, that it is I Myself" (Luke 24:39).
- To doubting Thomas, Jesus said, "Reach your finger here, and look at My hands" (John 20:27).

- It was this touch which precipitated one of the most unwavering confessions of faith ever uttered: "My Lord and my God" (John 20:28).

Look at your hands. Think how much Christ's hands suffered for your sake. Meditate on the truths in these lessons. In judgment, if God should ask you the same question He asked Moses: "What is that in your hand?" (Exodus 4:2), what will you say?

—Jane McWhorter

Note by Jane to the publisher in the margin of the revised manuscript:

> *I sobbed when I read the above text again. God has been so good. This has been a time of great blessings—eight books by me, one by Don and me, and two by other women and me. The book* She Hath Done What She Could *started it all, as clumsy as it was then. The dedication has special meaning to me. Oh, He has been so good. Who would ever have dreamed what would follow?*

# INTRODUCTION

Can you imagine the church without any organized programs? How many needs would be neglected? However, those who work only in these organized efforts miss the joy that comes from spontaneous service in His kingdom. Usually a woman who daily seeks individual opportunities to help others will also give her full cooperation to a formal program of work. This book is designed to help a Christian woman find more avenues of service.

The theme for our study is the beautiful story of the woman who poured ointment on our Lord's head and received His praise:

> She has done what she could. She has come beforehand to anoint My body for burial. Assuredly, I say to you, wherever this gospel is preached in the whole world, what this woman has done will also be told as a memorial to her (Mark 14:8–9).

Because of its beauty and sentimentality, the language of the King James Version is retained from the above passage in the book title: *She Hath Done What She Could.*

God does not hold you responsible for talents you do not possess, but He does expect you to use your ability to the fullest. Even if you are not capable of outstanding public service, there is something for you to do. Each woman teaches with her life, if not with her lips.

Too often we build our own prison walls with stones of doubt and fear of failure. We overlook the common, everyday things around us that may be used in His service. When Moses was making so many excuses for not leading His people, God asked him, "What is that in your hand?" (Exodus 4:2). He replied, "A rod." Only a common shepherd's rod, but God used it for the needed task.

Petty excuses for neglecting the Lord's work will not suffice at the day of judgment. How will we answer if He asks us the same question He asked Moses? We hold so many items in our hands each day—things that can be used to God's glory. How do we use our cooking utensils, our irons, our pens, our scissors and glue, our phones, our computers, our homes, our cars? Are we stewards of the material possessions God has let us use, or do we take selfish possession of them?

Service to others assumes a deeper significance when we realize this: Serving others is the only way we can minister to Christ because He is not physically present. Notice Matthew's comment at the crucifixion: "And many women who followed Jesus from Galilee, ministering to Him, were looking on from afar" (Matthew 27:55).

How gladly we would have cared for His needs had we been there, yet He tells us that we serve Him by serving others. "Inasmuch as you did it to one of the least of these My brethren, you did it to Me" (Matthew 25:40).

Through the years I have worked beside many faithful women in the Lord's kingdom. To them I say, "I love you dearly. You will probably recognize your own examples in this study. Thank you from the bottom of my heart for all you have meant to me."

CHAPTER 1

# ACCEPTING WOMAN'S ROLE

*Man was not created for the woman's sake,*
*but woman for the man's sake.*
**—1 Corinthians 11:9**

This book will not focus on what a woman cannot do, because her work is positive. She can perform many services more effectively than a man can. How many men can adequately care for the needs of the sick? How many men can prepare a meal to show hospitality? Some, of course. But the list is endless of works in which women excel in talent and experience. Man has his work in God's service and woman has hers. God in His wisdom defined both. In this first lesson only, we will study God's will for Christian women as they work in His service.

## How It All Began

Man was originally created to have dominion over lower forms of life (Genesis 1:26). God pronounced His creations good except for one thing: "It is not good that man should be alone," so woman was created from the beginning to be a "help meet for him" (Genesis 2:18 KJV). In other words, woman was intended to be a helper suitable for man. She was made for the glory of man (1 Corinthians 11:7). When a woman assumes her God-given role as man's companion and helper, she achieves her greatest sense of accomplishment.

Obedience is a learned, willful behavior—not instinctive.

The original state of perfection did not last long. As a result of the wiles of the devil and woman's desire for something forbidden, she sinned and was driven from the garden, her husband along with her, for he also sinned.

Man's punishment is given in Genesis 3:17–19. Hard, physical labor became necessary for man to produce his food. "In the sweat of your face you shall eat bread" (Genesis 3:19). God then pronounced the curse of death upon the human family: "For dust you are, and to dust you shall return" (Genesis 3:19).

Eve did not escape the consequences of her sin. Her punishment was twofold (Genesis 3:16). First, she would bring forth children in sorrow. Second, she was placed in subjection to her husband. He would rule over her.

*For a man indeed ought not to cover his head, since he is the image and* glory *of God; but woman is the* glory *of man. For man is not from* woman*, but woman from man. Nor was man created for the* woman*, but woman for the* man (1 Corinthians 11:7–9).

What are the two ongoing consequences of the first woman's sin? (Genesis 3:16).

1. Children in Sorrow

2. Subjection to her husband

## The New Testament and the Wife's Subjection

In the book of Titus, Paul tells the older women to be teachers of the younger women. Among other things, they were to teach them to be "obedient to their own husbands, that the Word of God may not be blasphemed" (Titus 2:5). Obedience as used here is a learned, willful behavior—not instinctive.

Peter further supports Paul's teachings in his general instructions:

> Wives, likewise, be submissive to your own husbands, that even if some do not obey the word, they, without a word, may be won by the conduct of their wives (1 Peter 3:1).

Notice that a woman cannot refuse to obey her husband because he isn't a Christian. As long as he does not ask her to go against God's commands, she must obey him, just as if he were a Christian.

Another direct command is given in Ephesians 5:22: "Wives, submit to your own husbands, as to the Lord."

Define *submission.*

How do the words *submit* and *obey* oppose the views of women in our culture? How do those views affect Christian women?

- Why must a Christian woman make a conscious choice to submit to her husband? What happens when she chooses not to be submissive?

## Woman Is Not the Only One in Subjection

Women need not feel that God is discriminating against them. In God's system of law and order, His wisdom dictated that one of the two adults in a home should be the leader. Two bosses create confusion. Man received his punishment for his original sin (Genesis 3:17–19), and woman received hers (Genesis 3:16). Part of her punishment involved being placed under the rule of her husband. Even if there had been no punishment for sin, doesn't it make more sense to have one leader so as to have order in the home?

God extended His system of order to relationships other than husbands and wives. For example,

*Citizens are subject to their government:* "Remind them to be subject to rulers and authorities, to obey, to be ready for every good work" (Titus 3:1). "Let every soul be subject to the governing authorities. For there is no authority except from God, and the authorities that exist are appointed by God" (Romans 13:1).

*Servants are subject to their masters.* "Servants, be submissive to your masters with all fear, not only to the good and gentle, but also to the harsh" (1 Peter 2:18). Note that it did not matter if the masters were unjust. The servants still had to obey if there was to be order in society.

*Christ was subject to the Father.* God's system of subjection even extended to the Godhead. "Jesus said to them, 'My food is to do the will of Him who sent Me, and to finish His work' " (John 4:34).

Note God's comparison of authority in Ephesians 5:23–24. The husband is over the wife even as Christ is over the church. The church is referred to as the bride of Christ (Revelation 21:9). The church is in subjection to the will of Christ, but His rule over His bride is one of love and tender concern for her welfare: "Husbands, love your wives, just as Christ also loved the church and gave Himself for her" (Ephesians 5:25).

## Perspective vs. Resentment

If a woman will look on her submission to her husband in the proper manner, she should feel no resentment. Instead of considering herself inferior, she will feel loved and cherished, protected from many cares of this world. Certainly no husband who truly loves his wife will make decisions affecting her without first considering her wishes and preferences. Under this system, children may grow up in peace and harmony instead of living in an atmosphere of tension and confusion which results when a husband and wife determine to move in opposite directions.

> Mob rule: Each person has his own way.

Notice the logical reasoning behind God's plan. Respect for authority is the only reasonable way to carry on any group activity. Mob rule is the result of everyone's having his own way. Witness it in our streets today.

All board members of a corporation are vital. However, if meetings are to be orderly, someone must have the final word, and that someone is the chairman of the board.

Elders rule over a congregation, not because they are so superior to the rest of the members, but because someone must be appointed to have the final word in matters of judgment and expediency. Reread the qualifications in Titus 1:5–9 and 1 Timothy 3:1–7. Aside from a few family qualifications, the things required of an elder should be found in every mature Christian.

A principal is appointed to govern a school, not because the teachers are his slaves, but because someone must have the final authority to ensure order.

When a woman realizes that she is not the only one in submission and that orderliness cannot prevail without God's system of authority, she should feel gratitude and not resentment.

- Name other areas of subjection.

work-
supervisor → Dept head → Division
in Flight - Stewardess → Pilot
Police - Judges

- Discuss the necessity for respect of authority in business, in a congregation, in a school. What is the purpose of a leader?

-Control - proper direction
- guidance
-vision
-Responsibility

- How has lack of respect for authority been a factor in mob violence?

Confusion - they become scared
Danger to do + protect
Others
Sin

## Women in the Church

Consider a woman's proper relationship to men in the church in regard to teaching:

1. The Greek word for "silence" in 1 Timothy 2:11–12 is not the same word used for "silent" in 1 Corinthians 14:34. The word in 1 Corinthians means that not one word is to be spoken. (In this passage certain men were forbidden to speak a word for the sake of order.) In 1 Timothy the word translated "silence" means "quietness." The same Greek word is used in 1 Thessalonians 4:11: "that you also aspire to lead a quiet life." It occurs again in 2 Thessalonians 3:12: "that they work in quietness."
2. "To teach" implies a didactic discourse. A woman is forbidden to deliver such a message or in any way have the preeminence over men. There are conditions under which a woman may teach (considered in a later lesson), but at all times she must remain in the place God has appointed for her.
3. She is to be in subjection and must not usurp authority over the man. It is more than a husband-wife relationship. It is a broad principle in spiritual matters.

The application today: In their eagerness to work and their impatience over men's delays, women have been guilty of assuming authority God has not granted them.

## Seminars, Ladies' Classes, Public Gatherings

While Christian women would not think of usurping authority over men by preaching, leading prayer, or leading singing during a worship service, women have, nevertheless, assumed a position of authority in a number of areas. Consider some of these:

1. *Teacher training programs or family seminars.* Some have maintained that a woman is not teaching a Bible lesson if the setting is a teacher training program or a family seminar. Instead, she is sharing her knowledge of visual aids or family life with her brethren. Others have argued that this is not a public assembly of worship and that she is free to teach both men and women.

   Think about these points. Is not a seminar carried on as a work of the church, paid for by funds from the treasury? Would the elders permit a woman to teach the book of Romans, for example, to a mixed class just because she had some special knowledge on the subject? Read the verses immediately preceding and following 1 Timothy 2:11–12. Is this passage not a broad principle applying to every phase of the woman-man relationship? Is a woman not assuming the preeminence and authority when she is in charge of a class?

2. *Ladies' class projects.* Most women want to be busy for the Lord, and it is logical for a ladies' class to share the work of the church. When the elders ask these classes to serve in areas in which women are more skilled than men, there is no usurping of authority. Women may even suggest things that the elders have not considered. But when ladies' classes devise their own projects, have their own treasury, and carry on their own program of work—whether it be benevolence or mission work—without the knowledge and desire of the elders, they are usurping the authority that rightfully belongs to man. Let us not be guilty of allowing our zeal to cause us to sin.

3. *Prayer in public gatherings.* In recent years girls and women have uttered all or part of the prayers offered in mixed groups. This has

happened in teenage retreats and in private gatherings of several families in a home. Since 1 Timothy 2:11–12 is a broad principle governing all phases of our lives, how can such a practice be justified?

- We have already studied that man is "the image and glory of God; but woman is the glory of man. For man is not from woman but woman from man. Nor was man created for the woman, but woman for the man" (1 Corinthians 11:7–9). How does this scripture relate to the three points listed above?

- Why would a Christian woman want to take the lead in the programs above?

- If any activity is questionable as to its being biblical, why would a Christian woman want to take the safest route possible? Why might she want to take a chance?

## Conclusion

A woman who insists on her own way is not a mature Christian. God made certain laws governing woman's place in her home and in the church. Aside from punishment for Eve's sin, there is reason and orderliness in God's plan. Even if a woman does not agree with the plan and even if she does not see the reasoning behind it, she must submit her will to the will of God.

Woman's sphere is not a prison cell where she must sit in idleness. Her domain is a very beautiful one. Instead of fretting about things she cannot do, a Christian woman should strive to do everything possible within God's boundaries. We have not begun to do half of what we can rightfully do and be pleasing to God. The remainder of this study is designed to motivate us to use our full potential in our rightful places. The ideas are not new, but they are workable. If just one woman is motivated to work harder in the Lord's kingdom, then all the effort connected with this study is worthwhile.

CHAPTER 2

# INCREASING SPIRITUALITY

*The mind set on the flesh is death,*
*but the mind set on the Spirit is life and peace.*
**—Romans 8:6**

Now we come to the theme for the rest of our study: The Christian woman and her relationship to others in her various fields of service. Before she can effectively give of herself to others, she must examine herself. If she does not serve with the right attitude, she is likely to become resentful of the time and effort she invests. But as long as her spiritual nature is in tune with God, gratifying outward manifestations will automatically follow: "For as he thinks in his heart, so is he" (Proverbs 23:7).

## What Is Spirituality?

We all say that we want more of it, but what is spirituality anyway? A dictionary defines it as "predominantly spiritual character, as shown in thought, teachings, life, or appearance; devotion to the things of the spirit." *Spirituality* means caring more for spiritual matters than for material possessions. Paul states it succinctly:

> For those who are according to the flesh set their minds on the things of the flesh, but those who are according to the Spirit, the things of the Spirit. For the mind set on the flesh is death, but the mind set on the Spirit is life and peace (Romans 8:5–6 NASB).

Our being is composed of two diametrically opposed parts—soul and body. If we emphasize our bodies and things pertaining to the world, we are carnal-minded. If we emphasis our souls and things pertaining to God, we are spiritual-minded.

Notice that spirituality is defined as your mindset as you fill in the blanks from Romans 8: 5–6 (NASB):

*For those who are according to the* ________ *set their* ________ *on the things of the* ________, *but those who are according to the* ________, *the things of the Spirit. For the* ________ ________ *on the flesh is death, but the* ________ ________ *on the Spirit is* ________ *and* ________.

Write a "C" in front of the statements that depict a carnal mind. Write a "S" in front of the statements that pertain to a spiritual mind.

_____ 1. If I don't show up at the musical event starring my boss's daughter, I probably won't get the promotion.

_____ 2. She usually is not that short-tempered. Perhaps she is suffering some crisis at home.

_____ 3. Whatever! He certainly has no interest in *my* feelings!

_____ 4. Well, she will never know that I just couldn't wait to tell that secret even though I promised I would not!

_____ 5. As soon as I find my Bible, I'm sure the Lord will have something to say to me about this problem.

_____ 6. Who cares what that old fuddy-duddy at church says about being modest? A little cleavage showing is all the rage!

_____ 7. I am tired; it's true. But one more visit may be just what she needs to encourage her to become a Christian.

## Proper Balance

God does not desire that we be hermits, not even to devote all our time to spiritual matters. Christian women live in the world, and they must devote time to worldly concerns.

The worthy woman of Proverbs 31 was certainly not lazy: "She watches over the ways of her household, and does not eat the bread of idleness" (Proverbs 31:27). That ideal woman invested time in oiling the wheels of daily duty centering around the needs of her family. Her attitude in these tasks must have been exceptionally reflective of her spirituality since her family did "rise up and call her blessed." Common sense dictates that if we devote all our waking hours to spiritual matters we would neglect the physical needs of our families. That would be wrong.

> Spirituality is defined as your mindset.

However, the other extreme is not acceptable. Devoting most of our time to the physical aspects of our families robs us and them of the spiritual aspects of life. Consider your activities in a typical day. Is most of it spent in routine tasks at home and work, plus driving your children from one activity to another? Aside from regular worship with the church, how many hours do you spend thinking about spiritual matters?

In the beautiful story of Mary and Martha, our Lord taught very clearly concerning the most important things of this life. Can't you visualize Martha as she hurried about the kitchen with the last-minute details of the meal? Can't you see the resentment growing in her mind as she watched that lazy, thoughtless Mary just sitting there listening to Jesus? She finally vocalized her frustration: "Lord, do You not care that my sister has left me to serve alone? Therefore tell her to help me" (Luke 10:40).

As a parent calms a frustrated child with firmness, our Lord answered with words that a Christian woman should read every day:

> Martha, Martha, you are worried and troubled about many things. But one thing is needed, and Mary has chosen that good part, which will not be taken away from her (Luke 10:41–42).

- The Lord rebuked Martha. What was her sin?

- How was Martha's complaint justified, if it was justified?

## You Can Take This with You

We sometimes say we can't take it with us, but Christ taught differently. Have you ever thought about death in this manner? When we leave this life, we can't take our homes, our clothes, our cars—things to which we devote most of our time. But we can take our own souls and the work we have done on the souls of others. Only spiritual matters will last.

Just what was wrong with Martha's actions? Shouldn't hospitality be a trait of every Christian woman? Evidently Martha's fault lay in her attitude. She placed more emphasis on the needs of the body than on the needs of the spirit. Mary and Martha are typical. The Marthas may be the first to have the visiting preacher over for a well-prepared dinner. The Marys, on the other hand, also gladly extend hospitality, but they take the time to invite their friends to worship and study God's Word with them in their homes and enjoy the fellowship of guests.

## Seed Chokers

We have numerous choices for worthwhile activities, but they must be kept in proper perspective. Membership in a neighborhood club may be enjoyable, PTA work or a career may be very constructive, children's ball teams may provide good exercise, an immaculate house may give a woman a sense of pride and accomplishment, but none of these things are the ultimate. Trivial pursuits can become so numerous that they stifle spiritual growth. Then they become wrong. In the parable of the sower, there was nothing basically wrong with the third type of soil. It was just that the thorns choked the sprouting seeds (Matthew 13:22). Too often our own thorns—cares of this world and deceitfulness of riches—choke out the good in our spiritual lives. We must differentiate between good and better. There is a magic word which can prevent our being pressured into many good activities. Try saying no.

Only spiritual matters will last.

Abstain from spiritual things for a time and you will lose your appetite for spiritual food. Those who habitually neglect personal Bible study soon do not care for reading God's Word. Those who fail to attend the services of the church lose their desire to worship. Those who pray only spasmodically lose interest in prayer. When a Christian woman removes herself from her source of strength, she soon dies. You don't have to deal a deathblow to a fish to kill it. You need only to remove it from water. You don't have to uproot a tomato plant to end its life. Simply block the sunlight and it will be dead in a few days. We teach the unbeliever that he is not saved by some miraculous experience, that only the Word of God can convert him. But do we sometimes neglect this fact? Only the Word of God can keep us saved.

Refer to the parable of the sower in Matthew 13 and notice the third type of soil mentioned. Summarize Matthew 13:22, then make a list of the thorns which try to choke spiritual matters from our lives.

Summary:

Thorns:

## An Empty Pitcher

A Christian woman is continually giving of herself, as does a pitcher filled with good things. If she serves blessings to others, her pitcher, if not frequently refilled, will soon become dry. Her myriad roles as wife, mother, teacher, personal worker, and servant in other areas of His kingdom will soon cause a woman's depletion unless she takes the necessary time to refill the pitcher.

If our lives are to shine, we must stay connected with the Power Source. An unplugged lamp cannot shine. Disconnected from God, a Christian cannot give light. Remember that we are the ones who stray. God is constant. He remains in the place where we leave Him.

Friendship is based on communication. Think back to your closest friends in your graduation class. At first you communicated with them frequently and personally. Now you leave short messages occasionally on Facebook. You naturally do not feel as close as you once did.

## Communicate and Meditate

For a mature Christian, prayer is a blessing—not drudgery. We talk with God constantly during the day, not just through a sleepy, dutiful prayer at bedtime. Just as we run to a close personal friend with our joys and sorrows, we rejoice with the Lord in every little blessing and tearfully cast our burdens upon Him when we are troubled. We talk things over with Him as we go about our routine tasks. He is our constant companion, so we "pray without ceasing" (1 Thessalonians 5:17).

However, prayer is only half of our communication. When praying, we talk to God. But how does God talk to us? He speaks through His Word. The only way we can remain close to God is by listening to Him. Too often we salve our consciences by dutifully reading a chapter from the Bible at bedtime as if there were some magical charm in doing so. We are not told just to read hurriedly through a chapter. We are told to "be diligent" (2 Timothy 2:15). Those at Berea searched the Scriptures daily (Acts 17:11).

Selena Campbell, wife of Alexander Campbell, wrote of their son:

> Dear Wickliffe, a lad beautiful in person, and lovely and interesting, both in mind and heart, was a child of great hope to father and mother, and gave promise, from his early piety, of being a bright and useful worker in the Lord's vineyard. So devoted, so consecrated was he to

> the reading and studying of the Bible that he carried it with him into the fields under his arm, and committed from its sacred pages daily, repeating the verses at night. It was the practice of both Wickliffe's father Alexander and his honored grandfather Thomas Campbell to read in the morning at family worship two verses, turn about, and then to recite the portions of scripture committed through the day (*Home Life and Remininiscences of Alexander Campbell* by Selena Campbell, p. 28, 1882).

The biblical principle of studying God's Word also has its corollary: the Word must have time to germinate. The Word is referred to as the seed (Matthew 13:1–23). A teacher who plants the seed on Saturday night will not see much growth by class time on Sunday morning. The Campbell family practiced keeping the Word before them during daily tasks. We need to get the Word of God into our minds and then think upon it. Let it germinate. Pull it out of the subconscious mind during odd moments. The insights gained are amazing!

## Minutes for the Master

We must truly take time to be holy. There won't be any time left over. Be honest with yourself. Have you ever been completely caught up on your many tasks? If we first do all the things pressing on us, there will be no time for God's Word.

Set aside some time each day for study and meditation of the Scriptures, and then work as many tasks as you can into the remaining hours. Someone has said that living is "so daily." God does not ask that our bodies be burned at the stake for His sake. In reality, what He asks is something that requires more courage and determination than a momentary summoning of our strength to lay down our physical lives for Him. Our lives are to be a living sacrifice (Romans 12:1). I believe it takes more courage to remain constantly faithful for a lifetime than to muster the one-time courage to be thrown into a den of hungry lions.

Public worship is essential and family devotionals are desperately needed, but each Christian needs to spend time alone with the Lord. Patterns of life vary. Some women find it best to take time at the close of the day. Others, unable to concentrate after a hard day, prefer morning study. Mothers with small children may find that their only free time is in the afternoon while their children nap. The time of day is not important. The important thing is to have a standing appointment with the Lord each day.

Charles Hodge made the following comments in one of his sermons:

> Does God expect to hear from me every day? Yes, daily. Praying daily does not require a PhD or a high IQ. About 5:00 A.M., God might be saying, "Well, it is about time for ole Hodge to be calling." Begin the day with God. Meet with God before meeting man. Solve today's problems before you run into them. When I get up in the morning, I look for God—for what He is doing in my life—because I want to be in on it. Give God control of the day, or Satan will take it. Bring God in; He will find His way out. Have a time. Have a place. Meet with God.

My practice of daily study / meditation during the previous week:

Review of Wed / Sun lesson
Reading of Muscle & Shovel

My plans for daily study / meditation for the coming week:

Feel I am reading & studying more in my life now.

## Bring God In

Learn to appreciate that the Bible is God's Word and that it is alive. Vary your method of Bible study. Read Hebrews 4 and underline verse 12.

1. Instead of merely reading a chapter a day, take just a few verses and really study them.

2. Run cross-references.

3. Read various commentaries and reference books.

4. Select and research a Bible character.

5. Study by subjects. (Study every scripture on the Lord's supper, for example.)

6. Keep a notebook on your studies and you will slowly develop a valuable tool to be used in personal evangelism.

7. Use a wide-margin Bible so you can jot notes beside verses of interest, reinforcing God's message in your mind.

8. Study a controversial subject such as evolution. Read everything the Scriptures say and then collect magazine and newspaper clippings. A year spent in such a study can supply you with a world of information.

9. Read Bible-related books in addition to the Scriptures themselves. Books on Bible geography and Bible history can add to your storehouse of knowledge.

Soon you will find yourself anxiously awaiting those moments each day when you can be alone to read and think.

## DON'T HESITATE TO MEDITATE

Plant seeds from God's Word in your mind at the same time each day, but remember that being spiritually minded involves more than thirty minutes a day spent with the Lord. It implies pondering your study all during the day. If you will only try, you can find many extra minutes each day to think about spiritual things.

Make use of routine tasks. Have you ever thought about how many hours you spend working in the kitchen each week? If you allot fifteen minutes each for breakfast and lunch, and thirty minutes for dinner, the time amounts to seven hours a week—almost a full working day. That amounts to 364 hours a year, the equivalent of nine forty-hour workweeks! If you think that number is unrealistic, cut it in half. Would that be more time in meditation than you are investing now?

> Being spiritually minded takes more than thirty minutes a day with the Lord.

You may consider the time spent doing routine tasks as wasted and begrudge it, or you may count it as a blessing. It all depends on your attitude.

After all, cleaning a kitchen is very mechanical. Your hands have performed the task so often they know what to do with very little mental effort. Instead of thinking of the seven hours lost each week, consider the time as a gift—seven hours each week for thinking. As your hands and feet do physical work, let your mind dwell on spiritual concepts. Be vigilant in looking for opportunities to increase your spirituality, along with that of your family. Consider the following ideas:

1. *Be thankful you are able to work.* When you become over burdened with chores, visit a nursing home. Then ask yourself how many of

those patients would gladly exchange places with you. The men and women who have to be spoon-fed and turned over in bed would welcome the opportunity to be able to wash dishes.

2. *Count your blessings.* Just for the fun of it, let each dish and each piece of flatware represent a blessing in your life. By the time you have filled the dishwasher, you will be a more grateful person. I kept the following verse taped above my sink until the paper became so frayed I had to remove it.

> Thank God for dirty dishes;
> They have a tale to tell.
> While other folks go hungry,
> We're faring very well.
> With home and health and
> happiness,
> Why should we want to fuss?
> For by this stack of evidence,
> God is mighty good to us.
>
> —Author Unknown

3. *Use the time to memorize scriptures.* We're always complaining that we don't have enough time for Bible study. Write or type a selected verse on a small card, and tape it above your sink. Spend seven hours a week repeating its words and thinking about its meaning, and I daresay you will remember it the rest of your life. Using this method, you can learn fifty-two verses a year. Did you memorize that many last year?

4. *Think about the scriptures you have been studying.* Bible class teachers should begin the next lesson's preparation as soon as the present lesson ends. They get the lesson in mind and then meditate on it. So as your hands perform routine tasks, meditate on the scriptures you have been reading. (That also applies to daily Bible study.) As the seed slowly germinates, you will gain insights that you often miss in a hurried reading.

5. *Pray.* Talk about your problems with the Lord as you vacuum, wash dishes, and make beds. Mention the name of every child in your Bible class. Prayer makes a difference. Don't forget to express appreciation for all your blessings. As your hands busy themselves in making a comfortable, loving retreat for your family, thank God for such simple things as clean, sweet-smelling sheets. I found this quote, and put it on my refrigerator door:

   I don't believe in prayer.
   I believe in God.
   Therefore, I pray.

6. *Listen to a cappella music.* Purchase choral renditions from a Christian university or a brotherhood bookstore. Those selections will cheer your day and sprinkle bits of spiritual truths throughout your house for your family to enjoy. Even better than that, sing as you go about your daily routine. For example, one morning concentrate on songs dealing with the birth of Christ. Then on another day center your attention on hymns pertaining to the Lord's death. While your body is busy doing what it should to make your family happy and comfortable, your mind can transcend the years and the miles and walk the streets of Bethlehem and Jerusalem as you relive these wonderful events once again.

7. *Make use of spare minutes.* Have you ever waited for what seemed like endless hours at a doctor's office? Instead of twitching and developing ulcers, spend what otherwise would be wasted time reading His Word or thinking about what you have been studying. If you are somewhat reluctant about reading God's Word in a public place, overcome your shyness by doing just that. You might be surprised how others will respond to your courage. Once you learn to concentrate on God with others around you, minutes spent on public transportation can also be put to good use.

8. *Take a hike in the woods.* Our metropolitan way of life is making it increasingly more difficult to find unsettled areas. Plan an occasional walk in the woods or some other unmarred spot in nature. It is so much easier to center your thoughts on spiritual things under these conditions. Many enjoy camping as a family activity. Take advantage of the opportunities. Get away from the folding chairs, portable TV sets, and the crowds. Family devotionals mean much more in natural settings.

9. *Sing with the family as you travel.* Why not keep a hymnal in the car and put it to good use. Singing keeps the children occupied and gives everyone a chance to dwell on spiritual thoughts.

10. *Create ways on the job to honor God that do not distract from your work.* A working woman may be required to give full mental attention for eight hours. However, if her hands do most of her work without much mental concentration, the principles discussed earlier will apply here. She too may tape a verse on her desk for meditation or subscribe to an email or other social network service for inspirational thoughts and scripture.

Consider the following story:

> A woman sought to improve her spirituality. She carried a small Bible in her purse. But she was reluctant to take it out for fear of confrontation. "This little Bible is a stumbling block," she observed. So she purchased a large Bible that had to be carried around—she was not tempted to hide it, and she was often asked to discuss it.

Compare yourself with the woman in the example above. How can you improve your spirituality?

## SAND IN OUR SHOES

Do you remember, back in the seventies, when Peter Jenkins walked across America? When he was asked what had been his greatest hardship—bad weather, hunger, cold, rocky roads—he replied, "What almost defeated me over and over again was the sand in my shoes."

How aptly this applies to the Christian woman. The things that most people normally consider to be the big problems are not temptations at all to the faithful Christian. Most of us do not have to wrestle with the urge to drink alcohol or smoke pot. We have no problem in remaining faithful to our husbands. Worldly entertainment has no real appeal to us. Church attendance is such a part of our lives that we would not dream of being absent barring an emergency. But, oh, those little grains of sand that keep getting in our shoes!

Many petty irritations continually try our tempers. Our children argue with one another. We take it calmly until the sand becomes so irritating that we lose patience with them. We ask our family members to please keep their things picked up so there won't be so much work for us to do. Their promises may be sincere, but when toys, clothes, and other belongings fall where they leave them, we sometimes speak a little too loudly as we stumble over shoes in the middle of the kitchen floor. No matter how systematically we plan ahead, something unexpected always happens while we're preparing our families to leave for worship. A perfectly secure button decides to come off at the last minute or a seam selects that moment to burst.

We also pick up grains of sand outside our homes. A friend unintentionally slights us, and we allow that annoyance to ruin our day. Someone at the grocery store rudely pushes ahead of us, and an extra surge of adrenalin prepares us for battle. On and on the examples could go.

How does a backsliding Christian usually leave the church? Compare her spiritual death with the physical death of a plant.

## The Woman I Want to Be

Sometimes when we read Paul's condemnation of the works of the flesh, we pat ourselves on the back because we're not guilty of adultery, idolatry, witchcraft—imagine that!—heresies, murders, drunkenness, or such like (Galatians 5:19–21). But if we read the next two verses, our failures cause us to hang our heads in shame as we realize how much we lack being a mature Christian. Every Christian woman should have a mental image of the spiritual person she hopes to become.

> But the fruit of the Spirit is love, joy, peace, longsuffering, kindness, goodness, faithfulness, gentleness, self-control. Against such there is no law (Galatians 5:22–23).

Honing the virtues in this text takes years of concerted effort; seldom are they mastered in a lifetime. Those little grains of sand just keep getting in our way. We may possess all the traits of the fruit of the Spirit to a degree, but we should not be content with being patient only ten percent of the time. Outwardly suppressing our bad feelings in an effort to display the fruit of the Spirit is as bad as tightly covering a steaming pan of water. An explosion is bound to occur. The only way to overcome bad traits is by gradually replacing them with good ones. In his letter to the Romans, Paul says Christians are transformed by the renewing of their minds (Romans 12:2). Only by filling our minds with spiritual thoughts can we ever hope to have them transformed. We are certainly not going to become more like Christ unless we take time to read and learn what He is like. We may discard our carnal natures and gradually assume the characteristics of Christ by lovingly looking upon Him each day through His Word.

Categorize the fruit of the Spirit in Galatians 5:22–23 as they relate to your own character:

| My Strong Areas | My Weak Areas |
|---|---|
| Love | Peace |
| Faithfulness | Self control |
| Goodness | Gentleness |
| Kindness | Joy |
| | Longsuffering |

CHAPTER 3

# HELPING THE SICK

*I was sick, and you visited Me.*

**—Matthew 25:36**

A man is usually at a loss to know what to do in case of sickness. Unless your husband is a very rare individual, he probably has difficulty even feeding his own children when you are in bed for a day or two fighting a virus. He is even more helpless in knowing what to do for a sick person in the congregation. Do you know many men who visit the elderly? No! There's nothing like the touch of a woman's hand in those times. Without Christian women, this phase of the Lord's work would be neglected.

Organized visitation is good, but a Christian woman need not wait until she has received an assignment in order to minister to the sick and elderly. Thinking of them should become a vital part of her life. Whatever her hands find to do, she should do with all her might (Ecclesiastes 9:10). At first her services may seem a bit awkward, but soon they will become second nature.

## Our Final Exam: Matthew 25:31–46

When a student is told beforehand what his examination questions will be, he is foolish not to be prepared for the test. Matthew 25 reveals part of the criteria for our judgment. Verses 36 and 44 mention the necessity of visiting the sick. "Visiting" in this passage is far more than a social call, just as it is in reference to visiting the fatherless and widows in their trouble (James 1:27). Think of Christ's compassion in ministering to the sick.

We are to visit—look into the needs of so we can care for—the sick, but it is up to us to take this broad principle and apply it to twenty-first century living.

- Look up the word *visit* as it applies in the Greek language. How does its real meaning affect your interactions with the needy?

- Follow the instructions below for a class reading of Matthew 25:31–46:

1. Divide the class into two groups.
2. One person from the first group reads verses 31–36.
3. The entire group reads verses 37–39.
4. Class teacher reads verse 40
5. One person from the second group reads verses 41–43 and then verses 45–46.
6. The entire group reads verse 44.

How does the reading of Matthew 25:31–46 as instructed previously clarify your individual sense of responsibility?

## Two Extremes

Our concern for the sick often falls into one of two extreme categories. Completely neglect them or smother them. Either way recovery is impaired.

*Complete neglect.* Some sick people are like sick dogs; they want to be left alone. If that is your attitude, your wishes should be respected, but don't assume that all sick people share your views. But many are ignored because of the carelessness and thoughtlessness of others. Ask the administration of almost any nursing home how many patients never receive a visit or never have any little "extras" provided for them. You might be surprised. Down deep inside, everyone likes to know that someone cares.

*Too much attention.* The other extreme often makes a person worse. Too much visiting, especially the social kind, can be quite damaging. We all have known seriously ill people whose well-meaning visitors advised them of an acquaintance who had died of the same malady. But even if the conversation is cheerful, the ordeal of entertaining a steady flow of visitors can be quite tiring.

- Assign two women the task of presenting each of the two extremes above—from their own experiences. Write an experience of your own:

## Middle-of-the-Road Policy

Somewhere between those two extremes, there must be a happy medium. Every time an announcement is made concerning a sick Christian, an opportunity presents itself. There is something you can do, whether that person happens to be a close personal friend or merely an acquaintance. The same thing is true of any sick person, whether in your neighborhood or in a nursing home. It is only in serving others that we can minister to the Lord (Matthew 25:40).

## Those Sick in the Hospital

The individual needs of the patient should be considered, and common sense should be exercised in rendering service to those sick enough to be in a hospital. The things mentioned below are common, and yet so often we are negligent.

1. *Prayer*—Every woman can remember the sick in her personal prayers. That seems simple, but how often do we do it? What could you do that could possibly be more important?
2. *Cards*—What if every sick person received a card from every family in the congregation? That would be wonderful! Even if you cannot

do another thing for the patient, you can show your love and concern with a card and a postage stamp. Our intentions are usually good, but we often procrastinate until the person is well. Keep a box of cards and some stamps at your fingertips to make your task easier. Sometimes it seems best to shop for a special card for a particular person, but if we do that each time, we probably won't send many. Just send a card.

A card is not only an excellent way to cheer the sick but also a way to train children to be thoughtful in remembering others. Let them sign and mail their own cards. They need not be expensive. In fact, often a hand-made card carries more meaning than a commercial greeting. Teachers of small children can let each member of the class sign a card for each sick person in the congregation.

Elderly people and others whose service is limited by physical infirmities often overlook this avenue of serving Him. Even when you cannot physically visit, you can say "I'm thinking of you" by means of the mail. I know of a woman who carries on a real ministry in such a manner. Her cards are made more meaningful by a personal note.

There is something you can do.

3. *Flowers*—It certainly is not possible to send flowers to everyone who is sick, and even if you could, the large number of gifts would be a nuisance to the one you are trying to cheer. But a gift of flowers is one way of sending a little sunshine into your friend's sick days. You may experience an even deeper sense of satisfaction if you send flowers to a not-so-close friend who has not been remembered in this special way.

4. *"No Visitors"*—It is amazing how many people think that a "No Visitors" sign applies to others. To enter a room under such

circumstances is the height of rudeness. We do a service to the ill under these conditions if we send a card.

5. *Visits*—Not everyone in the hospital is seriously ill, and the right kind of visit can be of help. Constantly looking at the four walls of a hospital room can become quite depressing. Here are some suggestions to follow when visiting.

    a. *Make the visit short.* Ten minutes is usually long enough. Five minutes may leave the patient in a happier frame of mind. It is better to leave with the sick wishing you had stayed longer than wondering why you did not leave an hour sooner. Just because you have dressed, driven across town, parked, and walked two blocks, don't feel that you have to spend the afternoon. Your purpose is to let the patient know you're thinking about him. If company is already present, take a quick look in the door, say hello, and leave.

       Put yourself in the patient's shoes. Imagine lying there and trying to carry on a conversation with a steady stream of visitors. Sometimes the patient's family members would like to have a few minutes in private with their loved one.

    b. *Be optimistic.* If the sick one looks terrible, she probably already knows it, so don't tell her. And don't lie by telling her she looks good. She can see through your hypocrisy. Compliment her with sincere words only.

       If one of your friends died of the same ailment, keep it to yourself. And don't say anything disparaging about her doctor. The patient needs all the confidence she can get. Surely you can think of something encouraging to say.

c. *Offer to run errands.* Sometimes the patient has a need you can provide that isn't against doctor's orders. Perhaps you could wash gowns and return them the next day.

6. *Sit up*—Customs vary in different locations, but a family sometimes needs someone to sit with a sick relative. Don't wait for an elder or deacon to assign you to the task. Offer your services to the family in such a way that they will know you sincerely mean it. Sometimes we offer in a manner that says, "But I really hope you won't call on me."

7. *Child care*—What a blessing to have friends who will gladly keep your small children so you may visit your loved one in the hospital. Not everyone has a parent living close by to care for small ones. When you offer, don't sound as if you're offering because it's your duty. Be sincere and your friend will know your offer is genuine. I well remember a woman who kept my small son during a time of need and made it sound like such fun that I caught myself thinking, "She had a good time. I ought to let her do that again sometime." We often deny others the opportunity of service.

   There are times when someone needs to keep the remaining children in a family when one child is in the hospital. It is such a relief to the mother to know that the others are being properly cared for and she can focus on the one who is ill. Even if you don't keep the children in your own home, you can help see to their needs where they are—clean clothes, food, and such like.

8. *Food*—When a loved one is in the hospital, family members can go by a restaurant or open a can of soup at home, but how welcome is the sight of home-cooked food. Don't wait to be told to take a dish to them. Out of the love in your heart, prepare something that can be refrigerated so you can drop it by for the family later. When people have to spend a lot of time traveling to and from the

hospital, they really appreciate a bowl of home-cooked beans. This is especially true when the sick person is a wife and mother. Don't always fix a dessert. People need plain food, too. A fried chicken or a congealed salad can be the basis for a meal. A platter of sandwiches will be welcomed. Use disposable dishes when possible and tell the family not to bother to return them.

Which of the eight options listed are difficult for you when visiting the sick in the hospital? Which are easiest for you? How will you put your plans into action?

## Those Sick at Home

Most of the things mentioned concerning the sick in the hospital will apply to those sick at home.

1. *Prayer*—This is just as important as for those more seriously ill.

2. *Cards*—We are often thoughtful about sending cards to those in the hospital, but we neglect the ones sick at home. Those long days wrestling with flu can be brightened by the thought that someone cares.

3. *Visits*—Visits in the home may be more burdensome than in the hospital. You must use your judgment. There are many lonely people at home who would welcome your coming by. But be careful. You might feel freer to stay longer, but the homebound patient still

needs to rest. There is also the extra work of keeping the house clean for company. It is usually best to offer assistance and not to linger and talk. In the case of those with a contagious disease, leave food at the door. Inquire of a family member about further help, but don't enter the house unless no one is there to care for the sick one.

4. *Food*—Concerning food for the families of those in the hospital, the same rules apply when someone is sick at home. How wonderful it is when a woman returns from the hospital to find the evening meals being provided by Christian friends for a week or so. Food preparation should be organized to assure balanced meals. But even if others are not participating, provide food on your own. It really isn't that much trouble to prepare a little extra when cooking for your family.

5. *Care of small children*—When a daddy is sick, a mother usually manages fairly well. When a mother is sick, a daddy's care of small children can be quite trying. What a welcome relief it is for a Christian to offer to take the children into her home until the mother is well. Even keeping small ones during the day while the father is at work is a great help. Too often we say, "Let me know what I can do to help you," and the tone of our voice really says, "But I hope you don't ask me." Be specific and mean it.

6. *Sick children*—It has been so long since some of us have been children that we have forgotten how much it means to a child to be noticed when he is sick. Children may be shut in for weeks at a time with measles, mumps, tonsillitis, or bronchitis. If you would like to perform a truly satisfying service, seek these little ones. Notice when they are absent. Ask the teachers of the preschool and primary classes for a list of those who are sick. The remembrance doesn't

have to be much. Children are as thrilled over the surprise of an inexpensive gift than something costly. Look around in the stores for dollar toys. Buy one when you see it and you will have it when the need arises. A giant candy bar or even a pack of gum makes an excellent gift. Every child likes to open packages, so wrap it. It isn't necessary to make a special trip to deliver it. Just drop the package by on your way to the store, or send it by one of the parents. You may even go to the extra trouble of sending it by mail. Children dearly love to receive mail. Cards mean a lot to them, especially when they contain a stick of gum or a dollar bill.

If a child is going to be in bed for a long time, a sunshine box will be delightful. Decorate a grocery box with crepe paper and get several of your friends or some teenagers to help you fill it with inexpensive gifts. Wrap each one separately and number it. On the first day the little patient opens the gift marked number 1, on the second day he opens number 2, and then sequential numbers on the following days. Now he has a treat to anticipate each day.

Which options are difficult for you when visiting the sick in the hospital? Which are easiest for you? How do you plan to put these visits into action?

## Mothers with New Babies

A new mother faces problems that merit special consideration.

1. *Visits*—A new mother in the hospital will probably enjoy your visit. Here is why. She has someone to care for her baby and usually enjoys getting "prettied up" and having people drop by to congratulate her on the new arrival. But make your visit brief. It might even be more convenient to visit her at home, but please think twice before you do. Remember, she may have been up half the night with the baby, and your visit may coincide with the time she had hoped to catch a nap. As the years slip by, we often forget how much extra work a new baby creates: washing diapers, making the formula, and getting the baby settled into his routine. Colic is often a problem during the first months. Strange voices and strange hands, though loving they might be, don't help the infant's plight.

> Please think twice before you visit a young mother at home.

2. *Special services*—Although social visits seem out of place at a time such as this, there are often many things we can do to relieve the mother's load. Washing and ironing, caring for the other children, and preparing food are appropriate. One woman told me how wonderful it was to have a dish of food brought before the baby was born when she really did not feel like cooking.

3. *Little remembrances*—Gifts need not be expensive, but it is always thoughtful to take some remembrance to the baby when you visit the hospital, especially if you have not already given a shower gift. One mother mentioned how thrilled she was when some friends

remembered her with a personal gift of powder or jewelry. It isn't the baby only that needs recognition.

Survey at least three new mothers. Ask them the following questions and report your findings below.

1. What helped you the most during the first week after baby's birth?

   Meals

2. How did a visit have a negative affect on you?

3. What advice do you have for women who want to help young mothers?

## ELDERLY

Many people are not ill in the sense that they are bedfast, but their days are very lonely because they are not as active as they once were and because they remain at home most of the time. There is much we can do to make them happier. Take note of the elderly in the congregation and in your community. Try to put yourself in their places and do unto them as you would appreciate having someone do unto you if you were in similar circumstances.

1. *Birthdays*—Birthdays mean almost as much to an elderly person as to a young child. Make it a point to find when their birthdays are and send them a card. If you really want to make someone happy, bake a cake, get several friends together, and have a surprise party. You may share the cost of a gift or let each person get some inexpensive

remembrance. Giving someone a party is an excellent experience for teenage girls, so you want to let them help plan it.

2. *"No occasion" remembrance*—It is a shame to confine our good deeds to birthdays and traditional holiday seasons. It is good to express your love by some little gift for no special reason. Homemade candy or cookies have a dramatic way of saying, "I love you and I care about you." Older people can become very lonely, and your stopping by means a lot to them.

3. *Transportation*—We take for granted our cars that provide us the freedom to come and go as we please. Sincerely offer your services to run errands or take an elderly person shopping. Remember that they can't get about as fast as you can, so allow plenty of time for them to make purchases without feeling rushed. Many of the elderly would attend worship more often if they had someone to take them.

4. *Home Bible study*—Infirmities accompanying the golden years of life may prevent some from worshiping as often as they would like. Have you ever considered going into the home of a widow to show filmstrips—any filmstrip telling a Bible story—or to read or discuss the Bible with her? How she looks forward to it each week!

> It is a shame to confine good deeds to birthdays and holidays.

5. *Get-togethers*—Happily married wives don't realize how left out a widow can feel. Most of our social gatherings are planned for couples or families, and the woman without a husband feels like a sore thumb. Try planning a luncheon in your home just for widows—they need not be elderly—and see how happy you make them.

Discuss the options above that have never occurred to you. How can you organize your time to fit visits into your schedule? How is doing nothing a sin?

## Elderly in Nursing Homes

Many in nursing homes have all the loving attention they need, but there are others who have no one to visit them or provide any of the little "extras" in life. If we will only look about us, it will not be too difficult to find someone to cheer up. Just because nothing is being done on an organized basis, don't feel that you can't help.

1. *Adopt a patient*—The administrator of most nursing homes can tell you about people who are being neglected. Visit one or two of them regularly, taking them small remembrances—powder, tissues, soap, comb. You may be the only one who remembers them on their birthdays. If the nursing home staff desires, you may wish to care for their physical needs, as well as emotional needs: bathing, feeding, manicuring, and the like.

2. *Special favors*—You may wish to ask some of your friends—don't forget teenage girls—to join with you in preparing fruit baskets, candy boxes, or tray favors for all the patients in one section of the nursing home.

## Emotionally Ill

Most of us feel more competent in rendering services to the physically ill than trying to cope with the problems of the emotionally ill. Even though we are not in a position to render professional advice, there is always a need for a listening ear and a sympathetic heart. So often people just need a listening ear, with the confidence that what they say will not be repeated. Many times their problems are caused by the fear that they are not loved and accepted. Show them you care.

- Research statistics about mental illness. What are the chances that someone in your congregation suffers from depression or other mental disorders? Why are mental disorders more difficult for us?

## WORKING WOMEN AND WOMEN WITH SMALL CHILDREN

A woman with small children who works outside her home will not have much time to do the things discussed above. A mother is doing God's work in caring for her children and must realize that her opportunities for service to others will broaden as her children grow older. The woman who works for luxuries does not have the same excuse as the mother of small children. Unless she is working for necessities in the care of her family, her obligations in serving the Lord have not diminished. There are several ways that the tasks of both groups may be made easier.

There is always a need for a listening ear and a sympathetic heart.

First, it is much easier to run a dish of food by the home of someone who is sick if you prepare it ahead of time. While washing the supper dishes, try baking a cake. Bake when you have a few extra minutes, and put your goodies in the freezer. Then on your way home from work, or whenever you're out running errands, it is very little trouble to stop by the front door and leave what you have made. After all, it is the thought that counts and not the length of time you stay.

A mother with small children may do the same thing. Her little ones are usually safe in the car as she takes a short walk to the door of the house. When there are no communicable diseases, it is all right to take a small child in for a ten-minute visit. (It usually takes that long for a child to begin to feel at home and start misbehaving.) If you have two children, don't go in.

Some young mothers make arrangements with their husbands to keep an eye on the youngsters while they take a few minutes on the weekend to help someone in need. Three young mothers may take turns. One of them can baby sit while the other two visit. The next time one of the others takes her place so she is free. In this way, you always have someone to go with you.

Just because you can't do much, don't wring your hands and give up. After all, the Lord expects only our reasonable service (Romans 12:1). If only we will open our eyes and look about, we will find something we can do. Have you done what you could? (Mark 14:8).

Compare your excuse for not doing something about the sick and needy to your reason for going to a sports event, a concert, or some other entertaining function.

What acts of kindness meant the most to you in times of sickness?

CHAPTER 4

# COMFORTING THE BEREAVED

*God will wipe every tear from their eyes.*

**—Revelation 7:17**

What a blessing to have Christ interceding for us when we experience the sorrows connected with death. Having lived on this earth, He can truly sympathize because He too knew the pain of losing friends and loved ones. He experienced the agony of death by crucifixion.

## CHRIST'S EXPERIENCES WITH DEATH

Proving His divinity was not Christ's sole reason for restoring life to the widow's son at Nain (Luke 7:11–17). Verse 13 states that He had compassion on her. A mother's tears touched the heart of the Lord.

Jairus, a ruler of the synagogue, asked for the Lord's help in healing his twelve-year-old daughter. Before He reached the house, the girl died. Christ must have seen the distress on the faces of the grief-stricken parents. Imagine their joy when He presented their daughter to them alive (Matthew 9:18–26; Mark 5:22–24; 35–43).

Fill in the blanks from Luke 8:49–55:

*Someone came from the ruler of the synagogue's house, saying to him, "Your daughter is __________. Do not trouble the Teacher." But when Jesus heard it, He answered him, saying, "Do not be ________; only believe, and she will be made well." When He came into the house, He permitted no one to go in except Peter, James, and John, and the father and mother of the girl. Now all __________ and mourned for her; but He said, "Do not __________; she is not dead, but sleeping." And they _____________ Him, knowing that she was dead. But He put them all outside, took her by the hand and called, saying, "Little girl, arise." Then her ________________ returned, and she arose immediately. And He commanded that she be given something to eat.*

From a Bible reference book, gather material to explain the mourning customs of Bible times, such as "the flute players and the noisy crowd wailing" (Matthew 9:23).

Jesus not only witnessed the sorrows of strangers, but He also experienced the deaths of friends and relatives. When Lazarus became sick, Mary and Martha sent word to their close friend: "Lord, behold, he whom You love is sick" (John 11:3). By the time Christ arrived in Bethany, Lazarus had been dead for four days. The Scriptures proclaim the compassion of our Lord: "Jesus, again groaning in Himself, came to the tomb" (John 11:38). "Jesus wept. Then the Jews said, 'See how He loved him!' " (John 11:35–36). How glad Mary and Martha must have been when their brother emerged from the grave.

Christ experienced death in His own family when His cousin John the Baptist was killed. After the disciples buried John, they "went and told Jesus" (Matthew 14:12). Evidently the Lord in His sorrow wanted to be away from the crowds, for verse 13 states that He departed by ship into a desert place.

> The Lord in His sorrow wanted to be away from the crowds.

Probably, Jesus lost His earthly father in death even before He left Nazareth. Surely Joseph was not living at the time of the crucifixion, else our Lord would not have placed His mother in the care of John (John 19:26–27).

Not only did Jesus experience death in the lives of strangers, friends, and relatives, but He also knew death Himself. As He entered the Garden of Gethsemane, there was a point beyond which His disciples could not go. He had to face His agony and death alone with God. Since He was in a human body, He did not want to undergo the torture: "Father, if it is Your will, take this cup away from Me" (Luke 22:42). "And being in agony, He prayed more earnestly. Then His sweat became like great drops of blood falling down to the ground" (Luke 22:44).

Read these passages relating to Christ's suffering in Gethsemane: Luke 22:39–46; Matthew 26:36–46; and Mark 14:32–42. Sing these hymns: "When My Love to Christ Grows Weak," and "Night with Ebon Pinion." What do the words *ebon* and *pinion* mean?

The death of Christ was necessary to free men from sin. Since we cannot truly sympathize with someone until we share the same experience, His suffering also convinced men that He had insight into our suffering and sorrows.

Jesus' friends showed genuine respect for Jesus after His death. Joseph of Arimathea begged for His body (Luke 23:52). Along with Nicodemus, he anointed the body with spices, wrapped it in linen clothes, and placed it in a new sepulcher (John 19:38–42). Mary Magdalene was so concerned that she, accompanied by others, went to the tomb before daylight on the first day of the week to anoint the body with spices (Luke 24:1; John 20:1). Jesus' followers loved their Lord and wanted to show their deepest respect for Him.

- When Christ learned of the death of John the Baptist, he went to a "desert place." How can we know when a grieving friend needs to be alone or needs to comforted?

- Why do you suppose Christ did not immediately go to Bethany when he learned of Lazarus' illness?

Cite passages from John 11 to show Christ's compassion. Why did He weep if He knew He would restore life to Lazarus?

## What Can I Do?

The very least anyone can do when an acquaintance dies is to pray for the bereaved family. It means much to loved ones to know that friends care enough for them to approach the throne of God in their behalf.

We live in a busy world. Everyone is involved with his own problems, and too often we are negligent in expressing sympathy. A visit to a funeral home takes only a few minutes, but our brief presence shows the family we care. How sad it is when a Christian dies and only a few families from the church take the time to pay their respects. It does not matter that the deceased was not one of your closest personal friends. The fact that he was a brother in Christ should cause you to feel some sort of bond.

*Oh, but I don't know what to say at such a time,* you may think. It is always appropriate to say, "I'm sorry for your loss. John was . . . " Mention some good trait the family can cherish. An abundance of words are not that important; sometimes they get in the way. Your presence speaks volumes.

Many people cannot leave their jobs to attend a funeral. It must be disheartening to a grieving family to see only a handful of friends—sometimes only five or six—at their loved one's funeral. We who are available have a great opportunity to comfort in such a time of great need.

Sometimes we cannot express our sympathy in person because of distance or circumstances beyond our control. A commercial sympathy card or a handwritten note can convey our thoughts. Do not dwell on the sorrow and emptiness which the bereaved must feel, but assure them that God will help bear their burden. If you have experienced similar sorrow, mention it. Tell them you are praying for them. If you have a pleasant memory of the departed one, tell the family.

## Thoughtful Acts of Sympathy

1. *Prepare food.* There is usually a need for prepared food for the family and out-of-town relatives. Most congregations have an organized program to provide food, and that is good. Working women can help to purchase the more expensive food items, such as ham. Keep something on hand that you can prepare hurriedly or have something already cooked in the freezer. Even when you are not asked to provide food, there is no reason you cannot take it on yourself to do so.

   Neighbors usually take too much food to a grieving family, so why not wait a week or two after the funeral to take a dish. By that time the family is experiencing real loneliness, and most people have forgotten there is still a need.

2. *Care of small children.* Offer to care for small children so the family will be free to handle the countless details that arise. Also, the bereaved will be eased if a volunteer stays at the house to receive food and handle telephone calls. Sometimes an unexpected death will catch the house in a state of disorder, and we can render a service by straightening up. If there are a number of out-of-town relatives, make your house available to them. Ask for a list of people to be notified and make the calls. Perhaps clothes need to be readied

for the funeral. You could wash and iron them or take them to the dry cleaners. Food is usually no problem, but check on the availability of paper plates, cups, and ice. Provide what is needed. If you are close to the family, go home with them after the funeral to help handle guests and take care of unfinished details. Take note of the many things to do and offer your services in a joyful way.

3. *Visit in following months.* Grieving families are usually showered with attention from the time of the death until the funeral. Then they are forgotten. The first few days after the burial, especially around dusk, the bereaved will be experiencing real loneliness. It is good to stop by just to say hello and offer to help.

   During the following months, be sensitive to their needs. Invite them out on difficult days, such as holidays, birthdays, and the anniversary of the death. Often an active Christian woman will suddenly be excluded from social functions when she becomes a widow. Be sure you invite her and see that she feels wanted. She may need transportation or advice in handling business matters. Most women know little about household repairs and could use your husband's help to winterize their home, trim the lawn, or make small repairs.

> Weeks later, most people have forgotten there is still a need.

## Conclusion

Look around. You will find many ways to say I care. Not only our lips but also our deeds can convey the message. The blow of death can be softened by the presence of friends. Let us do what we can.

Lee -

Jennifer - Mother
meice
Brother N law

Marty - Pet scan

Liz Thibodreaux - Pancreatic

Glenda - eye sight

CHAPTER 5

# HELPING THE NEEDY

*She extends her hand to the poor,*
*And she stretches out her hands to the needy.*
**—Proverbs 31:20**

Christians sometimes stress doctrine so much that we neglect the good works that will also be required at the day of judgment. Not only must we worship according to God's plan, but we must also give account for physical needs we have ignored (Matthew 25:31–46). Too often our attitude is that of Nabal, when David asked for food for his men: "Shall I then take my bread and my water and my meat that I have killed for my shearers, and give it to men when I do not know where they are from?" (1 Samuel 25:11).

> "I was a stranger and you did not take Me in, naked and you did not clothe Me, sick and in prison and you did not visit Me." Then they also will answer Him, saying, "Lord, when did we see You hungry or thirsty or a stranger or naked or sick or in prison, and did not minister to You?" Then He will answer them, saying, "Assuredly, I say to you, inasmuch as you did not do it to one of the least of these, you did not do it to Me." And these will go away into everlasting punishment, but the righteous into eternal life (Matthew 25:43–46).

Make a list of the areas of service which we are expected to render to the needy.

Relate the background for Nabal's statement (1 Samuel 25).

## GOD'S PLAN TO CARE FOR THE NEEDY IN THE OLD TESTAMENT

Instead of showing contempt, the Israelites were admonished to be generous to the poor and needy. Leviticus records specific instructions: "When you reap the harvest of your land, you shall not wholly reap the corners of your field, nor shall you gather the gleanings of your harvest" (Leviticus 19:9). Moses' law continues: "And you shall not glean your vineyard, nor shall you gather every grape of your vineyard; you shall leave them for the poor and the stranger: I am the Lord your God" (Leviticus 19:10). In Proverbs 31:20, the worthy woman is pictured as one who "extends her hand to the poor, yes, she reaches out her hands to the needy." And here is a beautiful thought: Ruth was gleaning in Boaz's field when he first noticed her (Ruth 2:5–6).

*For the poor will ____________ cease from the land; therefore I command you, saying, "You shall open your hand ____________ to your brother, to your ____________ and your ____________, in your land"* (Deuteronomy 15:11).

Contrary to receiving a shrink wrapped ready-to-eat package of food, how did God instruct his people to assist the poor?

## Biblical Examples of Organizational Efforts

The New Testament continues this same concern for the destitute. Why did the church need an organized benevolence program, under the direction of the local elders? Let's examine the Scriptures.

### Efforts within the Church in Jerusalem

Many of the converts on Pentecost lived far from Jerusalem (Acts 2:9–11), yet none lacked for physical necessities. Local Christians loved their brothers enough to sell their possessions and turn the money over to the apostles for distribution (Acts 4:34–35). The secret of their generosity is found in Acts 4:32: "Now the multitude of those who believed were of one heart and one soul."

> Macedonian churches "first gave themselves to the Lord" (2 Corinthians 8:5).

An organized effort was required to care for the widows in the early church. The apostles directed that seven outstanding men be selected to see to this matter so they could devote their time to prayer and preaching the Word (Acts 6:1–6).

1. *Collection for the poor saints at Jerusalem.* The saints in Jerusalem became needy. Paul instructed the church at Corinth to make a contribution on the first day of the week to care for those needs (1 Corinthians 16:1–3).

   Christians in Macedonia and Achaia felt a great debt to the Christians in Jerusalem because of the great spiritual blessings they had received through their Jerusalem brothers. In their deep gratitude, they shared their material possessions (Romans 15:26–27). Their liberality is even more remarkable when one considers that these people were themselves in deep poverty (2 Corinthians 8:2). The secret of their liberality is found in 2 Corinthians 8:5: "And not only as we had hoped, but they first gave themselves to the Lord, and then to us by the will of God."

- *Now the multitude of those who believed were of* one heart *and one soul; neither did anyone say that any of the things he possessed was* his own, *but they had* all *things in common* (Acts 4:32).

- Read Acts 4:32 aloud. Why do you think the Christians in the Jerusalem church were so generous?

  (one) vested in each other
  same like minds

- Write the secret of liberal giving below (2 Corinthians 8:5).

  1st giving of self to the Lord

2. *Individual care of the needy.* The New Testament gives examples of individual benevolence. The tenor of Matthew 25:31–46 implies one individual helping another who is in need. Whenever we see someone who needs food or clothes or lodging, we are to render assistance immediately if we are able. If our Lord were with us physically, we would be delighted to care for His needs. And yet ministering to our fellow man is the same as doing it for Christ. What a difference that makes.

   - *The good Samaritan.* Although despised by the Jews, the Samaritan was the only traveler who cared enough to help an injured man (Luke 10:30–35). The ritualistic Jews were concerned about obeying the letter of the law, but many felt no real concern for those around them. According to Jewish custom, if a wall fell on a man on the Sabbath, they could remove enough of the wall to see if the man were a Jew or a Gentile.

   - *Dorcas.* At her death, widows were at her house weeping and showing the clothes she had made for them. Dorcas saw a need and she acted (Acts 9:36–39).

What was the key to the Samaritan's willingness? (Luke 10:33).

Dorcas "was full of good works and charitable deeds" (Acts 9:36). How does this passage imply that sewing was not Dorcas' only benevolence?

## USELESS GIVING

Pure religion involves visiting the orphans and widows in their trouble (James 1:27). As we have already seen, "visiting" is more than a social call. James uses a word that means "to look into in order to help."

We must care for the needy, but if it is done only out of a sense of duty, it is useless: "And though I bestow all my goods to feed the poor, and though I give my body to be burned, but have not love, it profits me nothing" (1 Corinthians 13:3).

## HOW TO DO IT YOURSELF

Assisting an organized benevolence program—Christian women should give their full support to the organized benevolence program of the church. When called upon to help in any way, we should willingly give of our services, whether regularly bringing a can of food, donating good used clothing, sewing new garments, or keeping the supply room in order.

"Visiting" is more than a social call.

Another valuable service she can render is notifying those in charge when she learns of a family in need. After all, the ones administering the program are not mind readers. If they don't know of needs, don't blame them for not doing enough.

In addition to fully supporting the church's benevolence program, a Christian woman can do a lot on her own. When she sees a family in need of groceries, how wonderful it would be for her to run by their house with a couple of chickens or a ham—things they wouldn't ordinarily have on their menu. If she is a good seamstress, she may make clothes for the needy instead of turning the cases over to the benevolence committee. Frequently, a poorer family will need transportation for various reasons, and she may offer the use of her car.

Sometimes needy families need more than beans and potatoes. When a family has barely enough money to provide the essentials, toys for the children are out of the question. How happy a Christian woman can make children by giving them toys during the holidays or on birthdays. I have seen some very happy teenage girls, who, instead of giving gifts to one another during the holiday season, provide toys for a less fortunate family.

## CLASS BENEVOLENCE

The Scriptures give examples of a congregation's organized benevolence program and of an individual's caring for the needy, but classes that assume their own benevolence work from their own treasury without the consent and approval of the elders are usurping authority. That situation often arises as a result of misguided zeal and disappointment over the congregation's failure to have an active program, but all Christians must remain in subjection to the eldership (Hebrews 13:17).

## OUR BENEFIT

When we see a lot of suffering and so many people in need, we may wonder why God permits these conditions to exist. Of course He is omnipotent and could supply the needs of the poor. God is so powerful that He really does not need our contributions. Yet when we give of our means, whether to support the preaching of the gospel or to feed a hungry family, we receive the blessing of being slowly transformed into a more mature Christian by the giving of ourselves. It is really for our own benefit that God asks us to give. Don't look at giving as paying a price; just enjoy the benefit.

> I have shown you in every way, by laboring like this, that you must support the weak. And remember the words of the Lord Jesus, that He said, "It is more blessed to give than to receive" (Acts 20:35).

- Discuss what is meant by "supporting the weak" in Acts 20:35. Why could this mean spiritually weak instead of just physically weak?

- Share an experience of being blessed when giving.

## WHEN YOU WISH

How many times have you heard this question asked: "What about helping 'trashy' people?" We often remark that anyone can be clean and take care of his possessions. But before you judge people, try stepping into their shoes. You say that you would be clean, but have you ever counted how much it costs your own family each week just to remain clean—soap powder, bleach, dish soap, deodorants, toothpaste, mouthwash, bar soap, shampoo, paper towels, and various cleansers for the house? If you didn't have enough money to buy food, how many of these things would you purchase each week? If you had little education and came from a "trashy" background, how hard would you try to improve your lot in life?

When a woman anointed Jesus with oil, His disciples complained about wasting the expensive oil—the money could have been used for the poor. But Jesus rebuked them: "You have the poor with you always, and whenever you wish you may do them good; but Me you do not have always" (Mark 14:7).

We are familiar with this scripture, but how often do we apply Jesus' words: "whenever you wish you may do them good"? For some of us, we wish *never* to do them good. Often we do nothing because we are not aware of the needs of the poor. Or possibly, we never open our eyes to any opportunity to help. Maybe we do nothing out of fear for our safety. It's time to wake up to our responsibilities.

The following article is from an edition of the *Christian Herald* more than 46 years ago (January 1968), but it is an eye-opener as to what poverty is like.

## *You're Asking Me What Poverty Is?*

Well, you've come to the right person, but you won't enjoy my definition. Are you sure you want to hear it? Here I am, dirty, smelly, with no proper underwear beneath this rotting dress. I don't know about you, but the stench of my teeth makes me half sick. They're decaying, but they'll never be fixed. That takes money.

Listen to me without pity, now, for I don't need your pity. It won't help me at all, and it won't help my hungry children. Listen to me with understanding, if you can. Try to put yourself in my dirty, worn-out, ill-fitting shoes, if you can stand the thought, much less the reality. What is poverty? Poverty is getting up every morning from a dirty and illness-stained mattress—a hard, lumpy mattress. Sheets? There are no sheets. They have long since been used for diapers, for there are no real diapers here, either.

That smell? That other smell? You know what it is—plus sour milk and spoiled food. Sometimes it's mixed with the stench of onions cooked too often. Onions are cheap. We're like dogs in that we live in a world of smells and we've learned to identify most of them without searching them out. There is the smell of young children who can't make it down that long path at night. There is the smell of the filthy mattress. There is the smell of food gone sour because the refrigerator doesn't work. I don't remember when the refrigerator did work. I only know it takes money to get it fixed. And there is the smell of garbage. I could bury it, but where do you get a shovel without money?

Poverty is being tired—dog-tired all the time. I can't remember when I wasn't tired. When my last baby came, they told me at the hospital that I had chronic anemia caused by a poor diet, a bad case of worms, and the need for a corrective operation. When they told me about my condition, I listened politely. The poor are always polite, you know. We can't afford to offend those who might decide to be big and give us something. The poor always listen, for there really isn't much we can say. If we were to say anything, it might prejudice somebody with a little money. What good would it do to say there is no money for iron pills, better food, or necessary medicine? The idea of an operation is frightening even if you have the money required. If I had dared, I would have laughed. Who would have taken care of my children while I was in the hospital for a prolonged period?

I knew the day my husband left that he wasn't coming back.

The last time I left my children with their grandmother was when I had a job. I came home to find the baby covered with fly specks and wearing a diaper that had not been changed since I left. When the dried diaper was removed, bits of my baby's flesh were on it. My middle child was playing with a sharp piece of glass, and my oldest was playing alone at the edge of an unprotected lake. On my job I made just enough in a week to pay what nursery school charges for three children. So I had to quit my job.

Poverty is dirt. You may say in your clean clothes and coming from your clean house, "Anybody can be clean." Let me explain housekeeping with no money. For breakfast I give my children grits with no margarine, or cornbread made without eggs or oleo. For one thing, that kind of food doesn't use up many dishes. What dishes there are, I wash in cold water. No soap. Even the cheapest soap has to be saved for washing the old sheets I use for the baby's diapers.

Look at these cracked red hands. Once I saved up for two months to buy a jar of Vaseline for my hands and for the baby's diaper rash.

When I had the money and went to buy the Vaseline, the price had gone up two cents, and I didn't have another two cents.

– Poverty is staying up all night when it is cold to guard the one fire we have. One spark striking the newspaper we have on our walls would mean my sleeping children would die in the flames. In the summer, poverty is watching the gnats and flies devour my baby's tears when he cries, which is much of the time. I've never been in an air-conditioned house. I've just heard folks talk about them. Our screens are torn, but we pay so little rent that I know it's foolish to even talk about getting them fixed. Poverty means insects in your food, in your nose, in your eyes, and crawling over you while you sleep. Poverty is children with runny noses, even in the summer. Paper handkerchiefs take money, and you need all your rags for other things. Antihistamines are for the rich.

Poverty is remembering—remembering quitting school in junior high school because the nice children from nice homes were so cruel about your clothes and your smell . . . I remember when I quit and the attendance teacher came to see my mother. She told him I was pregnant. I wasn't, but my mother knew they wouldn't make me go back to school if she told him that. She thought I could get a job and bring home some money: I had jobs off and on, but never long enough to earn much.

I remember mostly being married. I was so young. I'm still young, but you can't tell it. In another town, for a little while we had most of the things you have: a little house with lights, hot water, and everything. Then my husband lost his job. For a little while there was some unemployment insurance. But soon all our nice things were repossessed and we moved back here . . .

Three years and three babies—then my husband decided to leave. I knew the day my husband left that he wasn't coming back. I hope he has been able to climb out of this mess somewhere. He never could hope to do it here, with us to drag him down. It was after he left that I first asked for help. I finally got it: $78.00 a month for the four of us. That's all we'll ever get. That's why there is no soap, no medicine, no needles, no hot water, no aspirin, no hand cream, no shampoo—none of those things ever. And forever, I pay $20.00 a month rent. The rest goes for food: grits, corn meal, rice, beans, and milk . . .

'Yes, I know there are health clinics. They are in the towns, and I live eight miles from any town. I can walk that far, but my little children can't, and I can't carry them.

Poverty is an acid that eats into pride until pride is burned out. It is a chisel that chips at honor until honor is pulverized. You might do something if you were in my situation—for a week or a month. Would you do it year after year, getting nowhere?

I leave my despair long enough to tell you this: I did not come from another place, and I did not come from another time. I'm here, now, and there are others like me all around you.

- Select two class members to present opposing viewpoints regarding giving assistance to "trashy" people. Write your own thoughts and suggestions below.

- Research in your Bible for verses that shed light on "the least of these." Comment on how a Christian is to treat the disabled and underprivileged. What scripture leads you to believe that assistance is a command rather than a suggestion?

CHAPTER 6

# ENCOURAGING THE WEAK AND THE STRANGER

*Strengthen the hands which hang down, and the feeble knees . . . so that what is lame may not be dislocated, but rather be healed.*

**—Hebrews 12:12**

Customs in Bible times necessitated caring for strangers. Hospitality was a way of life with those people. Today we seldom would be called on to lodge strangers, but society calls for other ways of expressing hospitality as we become plagued with a larger population. Our mobile society places many people in the position of being a stranger in a sea of unfamiliar faces. When a person feels that no one really cares, a crowd can be the loneliest place in the world.

- Write a few sentences telling of a lonely experience in a crowd. Share with other class members if desired.

## BIBLE EVENTS OF HOSPITALITY

What do we do when unexpected guests descend upon us? We quickly take advantage of the corner grocery store or nearest bakery.

But Abraham's life was different from ours. When he encountered three strangers in the plains of Mamre (Genesis 18:1–8), he could not run down to the local market. But he did have a plan for dealing with guest emergencies.

> Be hospitable to one another without grumbling.

Abraham ran to the strangers, bowed before them, and entreated them to remain with him. Poor Sarah. She and Abraham had to quickly organize their servants and begin food preparation. They had to bake their bread, kill the calf, dress it, cook it, and place it before the strangers.

So after washing the trail-weary feet of his guests, Abraham began his work. After a few hours of hurried activity, dinner was served, and the physical needs of the guests were met. The Scriptures imply no reluctance on Abraham and Sarah's part. Every act was one of love and joy.

In Leviticus 19:33–34, the Israelites were commanded to treat strangers as one of their own.

> And if a stranger dwells with you in your land, you shall not mistreat him. The stranger who dwells among you shall be to you as one born among you, and you shall love him as yourself; for you were strangers in the land of Egypt: I am the Lord your God (Leviticus 19:33–34).

In his letter to the Romans, Paul exhorted Christians to be given to hospitality (Romans 12:13). This same admonition is given in 1 Peter 4:9: "Be hospitable to one another without grumbling." The Hebrews writer says, "Do not forget to entertain strangers, for by so doing some have unwittingly entertained angels" (Hebrews 13:2).

First Timothy 3:2 states that an elder must be hospitable. Titus 1:8 implies that hospitality must be more than a duty, for a bishop must be hospitable, a "lover of what is good." Have you ever seen a man who could show such hospitality alone? If a man is hospitable, he has a wife who loves having people in her home.

In setting forth the qualifications of a special group of widows, Paul states that the widows should have given lodging to strangers.

> Do not let a widow under sixty years old be taken into the number, and not unless she has been the wife of one man, well reported for good works: if she has brought up children, if she has lodged strangers, if she has washed the saints' feet, if she has relieved the afflicted, if she has diligently followed every good work (1 Timothy 5:9–10).

Make a list of the qualifications for the special group of widows in the preceding text. How is this list a worthy guide for any Christian woman?

## Encouragement of Weak Members

We must never attempt to justify the negligence of weak members of the body of Christ. A Christian should be faithful to all phases of the Lord's work because she loves the Lord and wants to obey Him in all things. But before you so bitterly condemn the weak members or new members for their unfaithfulness, try standing in their shoes for a few minutes and ask yourself if you would do better.

While there are exceptions as to how weak and strong members position themselves in the assembly, let's look at a general truth. Weaker members often enter worship late and sit near the back of the auditorium. The more faithful members are at the front. When the service is over, stronger members do not interact with the weaker members because the stronger members are usually so busy. Sometimes the weaker members linger after dismissal, only to be treated as a piece of furniture as regular members rush to greet their special friends. How would you feel?

Members who are not regular in attendance usually know very few of those who are. They have no real friends with whom to sit. They have never been invited into a member's home, and no one has tried to become better acquainted with them. But we complain as we try to justify our negligence, "They never attend our potlucks." Of course they don't. There is nothing any lonelier than being alone in a crowd.

Write the name of a person you see occasionally at worship. What actions can you take to encourage her?

Only the Word of God can convert and keep a person on the straight and narrow way. A person who attends worship for its social benefits is attending for the wrong reason, but getting better acquainted with peripheral members provides an opportunity to get them to worship regularly, fellowship more, and study daily, and so strengthen their faith.

## REASONS OR EXCUSES?

Why do we neglect weaker members? Each woman has her own reasons, but most will fall into one of the following categories.

1. *I'm too busy!* All our frenzied activities keep us running. Ask yourself if all your "busyness" will amount to anything in eternity. Then think about the value of a lost soul. When you stand before the throne of God, all else will fade into insignificance: the club work, scouts, music lessons. The only thing that will really matter are the sheep who are on God's right hand because you cared enough to teach and encourage them.
2. *I have to work to make ends meet.* Is it really so much trouble to have people in our homes that we never bother? Some women are capable of simultaneously doing the Lord's work, running their homes, and being gainfully employed. Others cannot manage so efficiently and neglect spiritual matters for the sake of material gain. If a woman cannot work outside her home and continue to fulfill all her Christian duties, she should ask herself if she is working to provide her family with necessities or luxuries. She must choose the better part.
3. *I'm just not into interacting with outsiders.* Neighbors seldom know other neighbors, and everyone is so accustomed to going separate ways that it becomes a way of life, even among members of the Lord's body. Christians should enjoy the companionship of other Christians so much that their closest friendships are with one another. Too many members of the church have absolutely nothing in common with other members, and the only time they

> There is nothing lonelier than being alone in a crowd.

ever see one another is at worship or Bible study. If I cannot enjoy associating with fellow Christians on earth, how can I endure them eternally?

4. *My to-do list is already too large.* When we forget to put ourselves in another's place, we fail to remember how it feels to be the new member among strangers. So when we are "at home," we feel comfortable with our old friends. We would not intentionally be rude to weaker members, but we can be just as cruel when we thoughtlessly neglect them.

5. *Strangers, even in social situations, frighten me.* We are so afraid we will say the wrong thing or will introduce ourselves to someone who has been attending longer than we have that we crawl into our shells and hide to avoid embarrassment. When you honestly analyze an inferiority complex, you will have to conclude that it is fueled by selfishness. Instead of thinking about how we can make another person feel better, we think of self. We are so afraid of making a mistake that we fail to realize that the only ones who don't make mistakes are the ones who don't try. After you have introduced yourself to a supposed visitor for the fifteenth time, you will begin to learn to live with your lack of memory. After a while her name will be indelibly stamped on your mind. To be able to laugh at your own mistakes is a sign of maturity.

6. *I don't want to feel responsible for helping anyone.* Too many times we just don't love the soul of a weaker member enough to go to a little extra trouble. We may not love her enough to do anything positive to help her, but we freely use our tongues to criticize her. If we exerted the same effort in lending a helping hand, think how many souls could be strengthened.

- Describe the average weak or new member in relation to seating habits and acquaintance with other members of the church.

- How do you see yourself in relation to the preceding reasons for neglecting the spiritually weak? Which points fit you best?

- Make two columns on a page. On one side list the inconveniences in showing hospitality. On the other side, list the advantages. When we stand before God, how will our excuses look to Him?

## Steps for Strength

Here are some practical suggestions for strengthening weaker members.

1. *Speak to everyone you don't know at the services.* Even if the face is familiar but you can't call the name, introduce yourself and ask her name. Don't be so afraid you will embarrass yourself that you ignore someone.

2. *Sit in a different seat every week*. We habitually sit with the same group in the same place. In many congregations it has been more than five years since some who sit on the right side of the auditorium have spoken to some who sit on the left. They're not angry with one another; there's not a problem. Their paths just seldom cross. So in addition to becoming better acquainted with the weaker members by constantly changing seats, you will be surprised how many more strong Christians you will come to know.

3. *Adopt two or three families who attend irregularly*. Make it a point to become better acquainted. Sit with them and introduce them to others.

4. *Entertain one family each week in your home*, either for a snack after worship or for a meal during the week.

5. *Invite a good friend when you entertain strangers*. Select those who have something in common with your first-time guests.

6. *Rid yourself of the feeling that your house must be spotless for company*. The feelings you have when preparing to entertain guests are often transmitted to the guests when they arrive. Negative feelings make them uncomfortable. We need to learn the lesson our Lord taught His hostess:

> Martha, Martha, you are worried and troubled about many things. But one thing is needed, and Mary has chosen that good part, which will not be taken away from her (Luke 10:41–42).

7. *Treat guests as you treat your family*. Both you and they will enjoy the occasion much more. What makes us think that others always eat steak and roast? Do they never have simple things such as pinto beans and turnip greens? Do they never have sandwiches and cake?

What makes us think that other people live in spotless houses with no clutter?

8. *Watch for special opportunities for service.* When your adopted family is absent from worship, call to let them know you missed them. That is so much better than being assigned to check up on someone. When there is sickness, a death, or a birth in that family, be among the first to offer help.

Volunteer to diligently follow these suggestions for the next four weeks, and then report the results to the class. Write your intentions here:

Think of all the times friends have entertained you in their homes. Write about the situation in which you felt most comfortable. Why did you feel at ease?

If faithful Christians expressed sincere interest in weak Christians instead of criticizing them, the church would experience solid growth. Before you say "that won't work," at least try it. True, some people seem impossible to reach no matter what we do, but many will respond.

If you work with a dozen struggling families over a five-year period and one of those becomes truly steadfast in the Lord's work, isn't it worth all the effort? Think of the difference it would make if each of the faithful families would adopt two or three different families!

## Husband not a Christian

A woman with a non-Christian husband may be hindered in her desire to show hospitality. Nevertheless, she can do what she can. She might try working with a weaker woman instead of a family, using the same suggestions mentioned above. During the day she could more freely entertain guests than in the evening.

## New Christian

When a woman is baptized, why not have her into your home for a Bible study—video, book, whatever is available—designed for the new convert and invite a few other women with whom she has much in common? If you invite different guests each time you meet, by the end of the series the new convert should be fairly well acquainted with twenty women in the congregation. What a difference it will make for her when she enters the building for worship and many friends are there to greet her. Your thoughtfulness has helped a timid Christian to become grounded in the faith and given her a new confidence for worship.

Review these hospitality scriptures:

Romans 12:13

Hebrews 13:2

1 Peter 4:9

Mark 9:41

- If a Christian woman needs a Christian husband in order to be hospitable, then why does the Bible neglect that requirement? Write your other thoughts concerning these hospitality references.

> Help ground a new Christian. Give her a new confidence for worship.

## STRANGERS AT WORSHIP

We don't usually have the opportunity to take strangers into our homes, but there are other ways we may extend hospitality. How lonely it is to visit a strange congregation and be ignored. Maybe a few will nod or say hello, but no one cares enough even to ask your name. Granted, many visitors sit near the back and leave as soon as the final "amen." Members wishing to meet them need either roller skates or someone to run interference. But I have seen visitors sit near the front, exit at the end of worship, and get into their cars without anyone speaking to them. Shame on us.

An organized program for following up with visitors is good, but here are some actions all of us can take on our own.

1. *Be friendly and write down contact information.* When you see a stranger, introduce yourself. Of course you will sometimes be "meeting" a regular member, but so what? Just laugh over it and go on. Keep a small notebook in your purse, and have the visitor write

her name for you. If you both use social media, give her your information for Facebook or Twitter, and get hers in return. Writing the information is essential.

2. *Contact a first-time visitor within six days.* Many visitors do not bother to sign a card, and that's a good reason for keeping your own records. Follow up early in the week to let her know you appreciated her presence.

3. *Mail a note or a postcard if a home visit is not feasible.* Congregations often send letters to visitors, but a hand-written letter from a person is much more meaningful.

Some congregations identify visitors with name tags. One method of identification is to set up a table in the vestibule staffed by two mature teenage girls. When a stranger arrives, the girls pin a name tag on his lapel. At the end of the service, a designated person reads the names of visitors. Everyone likes to hear his name and to be noticed. That is only human nature. Sometimes we treat our visitors so coolly that we almost dare them to return to our worship. As servants of God, we must do everything in our power to make them feel at home and to let them know we want them to come back.

Make an agreement with three of your friends at church that you will all change seats during the services for a week. How many of you will find a new face or speak to someone with whom you have not talked in months? Report your results.

## Strangers in the Community

Most newcomers to our communities have difficulty adjusting. They feel lonely and are in special need of our kindness and consideration. Newcomers are often more prone to positively respond to an invitation to worship than are long-time residents.

In some areas a list of newcomers is available through various community agencies. When you cannot access a newcomers' list, however, the church has to rely on its members for such information. When a Christian woman learns of a newcomer to the community, there are several things she may do to show hospitality.

1. *Stop by for a short visit.* Moving is quite an experience and most people really aren't ready to entertain for several weeks. A short, get-acquainted conversation at the door is often sufficient. Let the newcomers know that you came only to introduce yourself and say "welcome."

2. *Take something fresh from your oven.* The ordeal of moving doesn't leave much time for baking cakes or pies, and your thoughtfulness will be welcomed.

3. *Extend a helping hand.* New residents need information about stores, doctors, and other community services. They might even need someone to run an errand.

4. *Invite them to worship.* Do so even without knowing their religious preference. They may not attend anywhere and would appreciate a direct invitation.

5. *Offer to take their children to Bible study.* Many families want their children exposed to other children and like the idea of their becoming familiar with the Bible.

6. *Inquire about having a Bible study in their home.* You may never have a better opportunity. If a home Bible study is not possible, offer to enroll them in a Bible correspondence course. Ask, "Do you feel that our neighborhood would be better off if everyone studied the Bible more?" Stress that the church is trying to get more people to study their Bibles.

7. *Leave them a tract telling about the church and its plea for New Testament Christianity.* They can read it in the quietness of their home. Your duty is to plant the seed. Leave the increase to God.

Study the suggestions for welcoming a stranger in the community. Try them this week and discuss the results at the next class meeting. If you are hesitant about any suggestion, write your hesitation and possible solutions here.

## Conclusion

Showing hospitality involves extra expense in time, effort, and money, although it need not be costly. It may involve a little extra housework before and after a visit. But the joys far outweigh the slight inconveniences. When the Lord demanded hospitality of His people, did He not realize that hospitality would involve some difficulties? Of course

He did. And houses during His time on earth were far smaller than our palatial dwellings, yet Christians were required to offer food and lodging to strangers for days at a time. It is sad, but often true, that those with the most spacious and expensive houses are the most reluctant to show hospitality for fear that their homes will get dirty or be damaged. The warmth and love in a home, even though it is small and inexpensively furnished, are far more important to a stranger—and also the Lord—than the chilling atmosphere of a mansion. Let us do what we can with what we have.

Amy's - DAD - Alzihemer's - Bill Hunter
Mom - SUPPORT

Cleo - Hearing
SANDRA - hospice At hom - Regina sis n LAW
NANCY -
Shannon -
wonder Camp -
Harold / Charlotte - both sick
Family Robin Wight

Chapter 7

# TEACHING CHILDREN

*Teach . . . your children . . . when you sit in your house, when you walk by the way, when you lie down, and when you rise up.*

**—Deuteronomy 6:7**

Some Christians say they are not cut out to be teachers, but if we do not teach in some way, we are defying our Lord's command: "Go therefore and make disciples of all the nations" (Matthew 28:19). God forbids a woman to teach in a way that is in authority over a man, so teaching children is one way she can fulfill her obligations (1 Timothy 2:12). Aside from duty, there is the real joy of teaching a young person.

A woman may teach her own children, as well as the children of others. She may teach in a formal Bible class or at home.

Think of the best Bible teacher you ever had. Make a list of that teacher's most outstanding traits.

## NO BOREDOM ALLOWED

A child learns of God before he can read the Bible. It is usually through some person that he first knows his heavenly Father, and you are God's representative. What an awesome responsibility! Therefore, the most important qualification of a teacher is that she really knows God as He is, that she is close to Him. If she has proper love for the Father, she will take the necessary time to study His Word, and she will find some way to get the Bible lesson across.

Every Bible teacher leaves an impression on her pupils, either for good or for bad. Some teachers may be excellent at teaching facts, but if facts are all they teach, they have failed. Consider the Bible teachers you have had through the years. You have to be thinking of at least one who was excellent. Perhaps she used no visual aids. Maybe her class met in a dressing room or a broom closet. Maybe she never enrolled in a teacher training course. But she loved the Lord so much and she loved those Bible events so dearly that you could almost feel the tremor as she unfolded the account of the walls of Jericho falling. Her Bible classes were not filled with dull and lifeless stories she told as a duty. Teaching God's Word was one of the most exciting and important things she had ever known. When she told of Aaron and Hur holding up Moses' hands in the battle with the Amalekites, your own arms practically ached with the weariness that Moses must have felt. Thankfully she knew that it is a sin to bore anyone with God's Word.

> It is a sin to bore anyone with God's Word.

Teaching is time consuming. It requires hours and hours of preparation. If only one of your pupils can face you at the judgment and say that he is there because of your teaching, it will be worth every minute of your years of preparation. You have no idea how deeply God's

Word may be penetrating the heart of that little freckle-faced boy who is always giving you so much trouble.

The impressionable years do not last long. While the child's heart is soft and yielding, much can be done with it—either for good or for bad. The way we bend the twig now will determine to a great extent the kind of adult a child will become.

I took a piece of plastic clay  
And idly fashioned it one day—  
And as my fingers pressed it, still  
It moved and yielded to my will.  
I came again when days were past  
The bit of clay was hard at last;  
The form I gave it, still it bore,  
But I could change that form no more.  
I took a piece of living clay  
And gently formed it day by day,  
And moulded with my power and art  
A young child's soft and yielding heart.  
I came again when years were gone:  
It was a man I looked upon;  
He still that early impress bore,  
And I could change him nevermore.

—Author Unknown

- Allowing forty minutes per class period, calculate how much time a child spends in Bible study in a year at the church building. Compare the results with the total amount of time spent on a school subject.

## Small Steps along the Way

A young heart is pliable, but we don't have very long to mold it in Bible classes each week—only ninety minutes each week if the child attends classes regularly. Little by little, however, that heart can be moved.

A Maine farmer announced to his family that he had finally succeeded in moving a large rock into the yard. Astonished over the feat, his son asked him how he managed to lift such a stone. The farmer explained that each day, as he drove the cows home, he turned the stone once in the direction of the house. It took two years, but the stone was moved from the pasture to the yard. Teachers may not be able to change a life completely. But by instilling the Word of God in the heart of a child, they may slowly accomplish something worthwhile.

We are concerned about nutritious food for our children, making clothes for their bodies, and keeping our houses clean. These things are necessary and should not be neglected. But when we allow things to consume all our time, we lose our sense of what is most valuable. Material things will pass. Material wealth, friends, and family can be taken from us in an instant. We will leave them when we enter eternity. The only thing we can take with us is another soul, whether the soul of a child, a husband, a relative, or a neighbor. How little time we spend on the one thing that is truly lasting!

> If we work upon marble, it will perish.
> If we work upon brass, time will efface it.
> If we rear temples, they will crumble to dust.
> But if we work upon men's immortal minds,
> If we imbue them with high principles,
> With the just fear of God and love of their
> fellow men,
> We engrave on those tablets something which
> no time can efface
> And which will brighten and brighten to all
> eternity.
>
> —Daniel Webster

## WHERE IS YOUR CLASSROOM?

When someone mentions teaching children, we usually form a mental picture of a classroom. That is a good teaching environment, but it is not the only one. We often overlook many informal opportunities to teach our own children as well as the children about us.

Study with your children at home. Eunice and Lois are examples of the effectiveness of home Bible study. In spite of an unbelieving father, Timothy was taught properly by his mother and grandmother. Those who are reluctant to teach publicly can teach their own children at home and perhaps even their children's friends.

Suppose our educators were to suggest that math is to be taught in the public school only one hour each week. Suppose they then announced that the completion of homework assignments is now optional. Every parent who had any interest at all in his child would rise up in indignation and protest that such a paucity of instruction could lead only to a generation of people unqualified to make proper change at the grocery store, to say nothing of the forthcoming dearth of engineers and mathematicians necessary to the operation of our fast-paced world. That is true. Good, consistent instruction and diligent study are required to equip our children with a necessary secular education. Even if there were no compulsory attendance laws, most of us would create our own. Our children would be in school regularly, receiving a basic education.

## What Is Your Standard?

Many parents do have a double standard when it comes to religious training, don't they? They feel that a diligent four-hour study of math each week is necessary to make a living, but forty-five to ninety minutes of religious instruction is sufficient to prepare their children for eternity. Besides that, many are not concerned enough to see that their children are present for even forty-five minute study every week. Our "most faithful members" are often lulled into a false sense of security because their children receive an extra forty minutes of class work on Wednesday night. When children who have been brought up in the church leave the faith as soon as they leave home, we wring our hands and ask where the church has failed. As necessary as Sunday and Wednesday Bible classes are, they are not enough.

> Sunday and Wednesday Bible classes are not enough.

Every time we read God's instructions to the Israelite parents, we should hang our heads in shame. Speaking of the required commands, Moses admonished his people: "You shall teach them diligently to your children, and shall talk of them when you sit in your house, when you walk by the way, when you lie down, and when you rise up" (Deuteronomy 6:7). As an added reminder, they wore frontlets containing God's Word on their foreheads and wrote the commands on their doorposts and gates (Deuteronomy 6:8–9).

Instead of talking of the Word of the Lord when we sit in our houses, we watch television, play with smartphones, and facebook our friends. How many times do we teach our children as we're driving them to school or to a scout meeting? When we lie down, we're so tired from all our frenzied activities that we skip Bible study. After all, the children are getting their homework until bedtime because there just isn't much time left when we get through with Brownie meetings, band practice, ball games, and music lessons. When we rise up, we don't even have time for breakfast before school, much less to begin the day with a study of God's Word. And so the story goes.

Using Deuteronomy 6:6–9 as a scriptural basis, research the religious training the Israelite children received. How does this compare with the training our own children receive?

## Transform Commands into Habits

We know the commands. "Train up a child in the way he should go" (Proverbs 22:6). We can quote 2 Timothy 2:15. Our intentions are good, but we can't seem to get around to Bible studies at home with any regularity. The responsibility for teaching the children is placed upon the fathers, but it is usually up to the mother to arrange home activities so her husband can fulfill his responsibilities. A wife without a Christian husband has to bear this task alone.

Why don't we study more at home with our children? Perhaps it is because the Word of God is not really in our hearts. In Deuteronomy 6:7–9 God told the Israelites to teach their children at every possible opportunity, but they were instructed in verse 6: "And these words which I command you today shall be in your heart." When we are overflowing with zeal to study God's Word, teaching our children becomes second nature. The Israelites were commanded in Exodus 13:8 to explain their observance of the Passover to their children. Perhaps the reason we can't explain our actions to our children is that we are not doing anything. Probably most of our neglect is due to thoughtlessness and a lack of planning to find time.

Each home has its own pattern of activities, and a suitable time will vary from family to family. School and work usually rule out daytime Bible study, but the family is usually together immediately after breakfast, after the evening meal, and at bedtime. Some families find that ten or fifteen minutes after breakfast is best. The few extra minutes of lost sleep are such a small price to pay for beginning the day with your family with an open Bible. If some of your family members are not hurrying to appointments after supper or if you are not exhausted at bedtime, those times might be best for you. Fix a time and make family study a regular occurrence. And be patient while all the family members develop the habit.

Select a time best suited to your family for daily Bible study. How will you stay motivated and committed to develop commands into habit?

Find at least two scriptures that indicate the serious nature of teaching your own children. How is this accountability often shirked in favor of scholastics, sports, or entertainment?

## Stages of Study

1. *Babyhood*—Never underestimate the ability of a baby to learn. Because he cannot verbally communicate does not mean he is too young to learn about God. During the first two years of his life, the baby is storing up concepts that he will soon verbalize, and we are delighted when his ability to speak suddenly comes. He does not learn to talk overnight. The process begins at birth.

   While a baby is busy learning the concept of "ball" and "feet," he also begins to form lifetime concepts of God. Before the baby learns to talk, talk to him about God: "God made it"; "God loves you"; "We love Jesus very much." Read books to him about Bible characters as soon as he can sit in your lap. He may not understand the words, but he soon learns that this activity is important. He also enjoys the closeness to you.

   Begin taking your baby regularly to worship when he is only a few weeks old. Although he is too young to realize what is going on, he learns that worship is important and is expected of us.

2. *Early childhood*—During this stage, most Christian mothers faithfully read a Bible story every night at bedtime. This is good, but do more than just read it. Invest in visual aids and make the stories live! We buy all sorts of material things—tricycles, balls, dolls. Why not invest in aids to help us teach spiritual truths? These early years are the time to teach children to sing and pray.

3. *Middle childhood*—Available activities for spiritual growth multiply as children grow older. During the middle childhood years the children are capable of much deeper Bible study. That is an ideal time for family study if the father is a Christian. The following suggestions may be helpful.

   A. *Select a Bible character or subject. Let the children take turns selecting a Bible character or subject to study.*

      - Locate all the scriptures you can find concerning that character and read a portion each day.
      - After the reading, let each member of the family ask the others questions about the passages just read.
      - Shop for visual aids on that character—flannel-graphs, coloring books, and the like. Use them as you study.
      - At the end of the study, review by writing the main events in the life of that person on small cards and letting each member of the family draw one. Each one sees if he can tell the highlights of the event on his card in his own words. Or write questions on cards for everyone to draw and answer.
      - Make a contest out of the activity by keeping score.

It is a good idea to locate the character on a timeline so he can be fitted in his proper historical niche. By concentrating on a character like this, it is amazing how everyone begins to feel as if he really knows the Bible person.

*B. Memorize. Don't forget to include regular memory work.*

- Write the selected verse on a large card and review it daily for two weeks.
- At the end of that period the verse will be indelibly stamped on the children's minds.
- Review previously learned verses once a month to refresh their memory.
- The verses can be made more meaningful, if you allow the children to draw illustrations on each memory card.
- Select significant verses which will enable your children to defend their faith throughout life.

*C. Bible games. Various games and cards can be useful in reviewing Bible questions in an interesting manner. These games can be made at home or purchased at a bookstore. Free games may be available online.*

4. *Teen years*—As children grow older, many families neglect Bible study. Most teens are engaged in so many activities that it is very difficult for all family members to stop at the same time for Bible study. But the family needs to study together more than ever during these trying years.

   The teen stage is an ideal time for in-depth studies. Select a subject to study for a month, the Lord's supper, for example. Read and discuss appropriate scriptures. Keep a notebook. What a valuable aid that notebook can be as our children defend their faith among their peers. Commercial workbooks can be very useful in such a study. Just ten or fifteen minutes a day can produce amazing results.

Remember, opportunities will surface that promote Bible study indirectly. An organized sit-down family Bible study is not the only way to home-train your children. Spend precious moments talking about Bible truths as you work together in the kitchen. One little girl remarked to her mother that bedtime was best because that was the time when she and her mother "just talked" about the events of the day. When lines of communication remain open between mother and child, Bible principles can be applied to petty irritations at school.

- Find at least two other Christian women who are dedicated to home Bible teaching. Swap ideas, games, websites, and even visual aids. Establish a group on Facebook or email, and correspond often. Meet at least once a month in person. How can networking improve your family study time?

## GRANDCHILDREN, NEIGHBORHOOD CHILDREN, AND FRIENDS' CHILDREN

A grandmother is special because she is related to a child but not usually responsible for her. Sometimes she can have a greater influence than the child's own mother. When your grandchildren visit you, don't spend all your time cooking and caring for their physical needs. Have a Bible story period and soon they will be looking forward to studying with you regularly. The same principles discussed earlier apply in this situation.

Then what about the child next door or down the street? Christian women who do not use the opportunity to teach Bible classes in their homes for neighborhood children are missing an ideal opportunity. Often a parent will let his child study in your home when he would not permit him to attend church Bible class. Saturday is an ideal time during school months, but any weekday may be suitable during the summer.

One woman gathered all the neighborhood children under a large oak tree in her yard one day a week during the summer. The children looked forward to their weekly Bible story and many who would never have gone to the church building attended. Only eternity can tell how much good was accomplished. This is an excellent way for teenage girls to teach smaller children in their neighborhoods.

You probably have friends in the church and friends from other walks of life that will welcome your time investment in their children. Not all teaching has to be done in a classroom. As you go about your Christian duties—visiting the sick or the elderly, preparing food for those in need—take one or two teenage girls, or even smaller children with you. They will welcome the opportunity and will learn some valuable lessons related to the role of a mature Christian woman.

List the approximate number of children in your general neighborhood, their ages, and their regularity in attending any classes of their own religion. How can you obey the great commission in teaching these children?

CHAPTER 8

# REACHING THE LOST

*For the message of the cross is foolishness to those who are perishing, but to us who are being saved it is the power of God.*

**—1 Corinthians 1:18**

Do we really believe that everyone who does not accept God's plan of salvation will be lost? Do we really care? Does it bother us that during the next twenty-four hours 157,000 people will die unprepared?

We say we care, but our actions often contradict what our lips utter. How long has it been since we talked with someone about her soul? On the day of judgment, how many of our friends will look at us and accusingly voice the sentiments of the song, "You Never Mentioned Him to Me"? Oh, we talk to them about recipes, clothes, childrearing, and even politics, but we never get around to discussing their souls.

So many have been baptized without being converted. Real soul winners believe that those who have not been converted—and that includes Bible baptism—will be lost. They love their fellowman so much that they can't bear to see that happen.

Answer honestly. Do you really believe that everyone who does not accept God's plan of salvation will be lost? How many of your acquaintances are in this category? What are you doing about it?

> Go therefore and make disciples of all the nations, baptizing them in the name of the Father and of the Son and of the Holy Spirit, teaching them to observe all things that I have commanded you (Matthew 28:19–20).

During what phase of Christ's ministry did He issue this great commission? How do we usually treat the request of a person at that point in his life?

## Positive Commands and Examples

How many ways may a Christian woman reach the lost? How many women are sending their souls to hell by doing nothing? We are often guilty of retreating to a comfortable hiding place when we say, "Let the men do it," or "That's a man's work." Let's explore the issue from the Bible.

What do you think Matthew 28:19 means? Do you feel an obligation to participate in the task of telling the entire world about Christ? Do you suppose the Christian women in New Testament times kept silent about their knowledge of Jesus?

Titus 2:3–4 authorizes a woman to teach younger women:

> The older women likewise, that they be reverent in behavior, not slanderers, not given to much wine, teachers of good things—that they admonish the young women to love their husbands, to love their children.

Aquila and Priscilla jointly taught Apollos when they discovered he was preaching error (Acts 18:24–26).

> When Aquila and Priscilla heard him, they took him aside and explained to him the way of God more accurately (Acts 18:26).

## MORE THAN AN INVITATION IS NEEDED

If we are going to reach the world with the gospel, we must do more than invite people to a church service. Surveys show that ninety-seven percent of those invited never attend.

Put yourself in an unbeliever's shoes and try to imagine how uncomfortable she feels.

1. What emotions might your guest experience when she enters the auditorium? Does she think she about to worship or attend a party?
2. What will she think about the way worship begins? Does worship begin with worship or with long and personal announcements in which she has no interest? Will she think the man who rises first is a worship leader or a comedian?
3. How will she react to a cappella singing?
4. How would she process "He Bore It All" or "O Sacred Head Now Wounded"?
5. And then there's the Lord's supper. Does she think, *What is it?* or does she wonder, *Should I partake of this since I am not a member?*

6. What can you do to prepare your guest so she will know she is on Planet Earth instead of Mars.

The entire world is our concern, but our own community is our special responsibility. We must find a way to reach our neighbors in more ways than bringing them into the assembly. Drive through the familiar streets of your neighborhood, and imagine what is behind all those closed doors. Where is their eternity? Many of them when approached for Bible study will be quite rude. Others will be polite but indifferent. But behind one of those closed door there is a Lydia or a Philippian jailer just waiting to learn the truth.

The Lord does not hold us responsible for those who will not listen, but we must give an account for the honest hearts we are not trying to reach. Do not try to determine who will and who will not accept the truth. Sometimes we dismiss a wicked and worldly minded person as an unlikely prospect, feeling that the Word of God has no power to change them. But the Word of God inside a person can change the heart of the vilest person. Try to get it there, and then let God take care of the increase.

- Conduct your own neighborhood survey asking at least ten people only one question: "How many people in our neighborhood have asked you if you'd like to study the Bible?" What are your results?

- Ask Christians you know, "Were you converted from denominationalism?" If the answer is yes, ask them to describe their feelings about their first time to worship with the Lord's church. Share that response below.

Paul was converted from Judaism. What was his heart's desire as a Christian? (Romans 10:1) What is my heart's desire for my non-Christian friends?

## Excuses

Our excuses for failing to reach the lost are myriad, but how will they sound on the day of judgment when we stand in the presence of Christ, who gave so much for lost souls?

1. *I don't know enough.* Studying is hard work and time consuming, but we have time for the things we really want to do. Anyway, "I don't know enough" is a ridiculous statement for a Christian of twenty years. Nowadays you can teach others if you know how to insert a DVD into a player.

2. *I am afraid someone will ask a question I can't answer.* That probably will happen, so what should you do about it?

   First, carry a small loose-leaf notebook in your purse. Do your own personal studying by subject matter and keep a record of scriptures, listed by topic. Write the entire verse in your notebook, not just the reference. That will help you to identify a needed verse quickly.

   Second, when the question cannot be answered by using your reference book, be honest and say, "I will have to do some more studying on that." That might help your relationship with the prospect, because most people are reluctant to study with someone who thinks she knows all the answers. You can search together for an answer.

3. *I don't have time.* Of course you don't. Your days are filled to capacity. Honestly, have you ever been "caught up"? Has there ever been a time when all the ironing, all the mending, and all the deep cleaning were done? If you have, I would love to meet you and congratulate you. Since we can never catch up, we will have to set aside time to do the most important work and then work in all our material duties the best we can. That doesn't mean we should neglect our families but that we must become a little better organized. At the beginning of each week, list the things you plan to do in His service during the next seven days—the prospects to teach, the sick to visit, and the absentees and visitors to contact. A list will help you to work these people into your schedule. There is no need to set aside an entire day for such work. Just drop by on your way to the store or while you are running errands. Reflect on your work at the end of a month, and you will be surprised how many people you have visited. Remember, saving souls is the most important work in this world.

4. *I'll get my feelings hurt when people won't listen.* Many won't listen and, if you are the sensitive type, you will get your feelings crushed at regular intervals. But remember this: You are responsible only for those who will listen. Don't consider a refusal as a personal affront. Read and reread the parable of the sower (Matthew 13:1–9, 18–23). Too many of us become discouraged when a prospect does not respond positively to the gospel. Then we ourselves fail; we fail to keep on trying. A salesman doesn't expect to make a sale at every door, but he knows an increase in the number of contacts will increase the number of sales. As for our work in God's kingdom, two or three attempts are just not enough.

   When we are afraid we will get our feelings hurt, we are more concerned over what people will think than what Christ thinks. Isn't that true selfishness? When we love Christ enough to put Him first, He has become more important than our egos.

Psalm 118:6 encourages, "The Lord is on my side; I will not fear. What can man do to me?" In addition, write the key thoughts of these passages:

Deuteronomy 31:6

Psalm 27:1

2 Timothy 1:7

1 Peter 3:13–14

How do these scripture relate to my excuses?

## Mention Him to Someone

Build up your confidence. That may be difficult, but hanging on the cross was also difficult. You will often feel completely inadequate. If you lack confidence, learn to talk to others simply about Christ instead of plunging headlong into a deep Bible discussion.

- Mention something interesting from your own Bible study to your friends so they will know you study your Bible. How tragic when our daily associates never even suspect that we read our Bibles or care anything about the Lord.
- Use statements such as, "The Lord willing, I'll do so and so." Mention an interesting statement you heard in a sermon.
- Let others know you are praying for them. If our actions do not support our words, our friends will laugh at us and call us hypocrites.

These measures are not meant to call attention to our righteousness but to let others know we are sincerely interested in them and place great value upon living a Christian life.

If you can't bring yourself to talk face-to-face with a friend about the Bible, at least leave tracts in public places—restaurants and waiting rooms, for a start. Many of them will be tossed into a trash can but some will be read, and you will be teaching indirectly.

How can Philippians 4:13 help to increase your confidence?

> Learn to talk to others simply about Christ.

Do friends, acquaintances, and relatives make good prospects? How often we overlook those closest to us! *They won't study the Bible with us,* we think, so we never bother to ask. Some of them may surprise you. Isn't it worth a try?

Newcomers to the community are especially receptive. A new environment presents traumatic experience. Old ties have been broken and newcomers are especially appreciative of any kindnesses shown them as they try to make new friends. They are more likely to agree to a Bible study more quickly than a ten-year neighbor down the street.

Review the suggestions for welcoming newcomers in Chapter 5. Write the suggestions you wish to follow here:

If newcomers to your area reject the opportunity to study the Bible or worship with the church, that is their decision. They, not you, will have to give an account to God for their refusal.

## Door Knocking

Have you tried door-to-door work? Who, me? Go up to a complete stranger's door and ask her to study the Bible? Yes, you! If you don't, who will? How are you going to find the Lydias in your neighborhood unless you search for them? Don't say that it won't work unless you have tried it. I was skeptical before I started to knock on strangers' doors. *People will never agree to study the Bible with a stranger,* I thought, but they do. You might be surprised how many will say yes.

> Be diligent about sowing the seed and let God take care of the responses.

In a town of seven thousand, one mission effort enrolled more than seven hundred in Bible correspondence courses and home Bible studies. You might be thinking, *Not all of those were genuinely interested,* and, of course, you are right. But if only one of them learned and accepted the truth, would it not be worth all our efforts? Did God ever tell us to be concerned about how many baptisms resulted from our teaching? Let's be diligent about sowing the seed and let God take care of the responses.

Door-to-door work is usually done as an organized effort of the church. Most of the time it will take the form of a religious survey, including questions concerning correspondence courses and home Bible studies.

If the church has no such program, we can still work individually, if the work is carefully planned. But exercise your wisdom. It is not wise for a woman to work alone in strange neighborhoods. We need to travel in pairs and conduct the Lord's business on front porches. Even then it would seem unwise for two Christian women to undertake such a task without the knowledge and approval of the elders. Most elders would welcome such activities. They are constantly searching for new prospects anyway. If you find a woman who is willing to study, you could assume the task yourself. If a husband and wife are the prospects, a teaching couple is a better choice.

Teens do well in door-to-door work. The public is generally more receptive to a clean, wholesome young person who is interested in serving the Lord than to an older person. Most adults hate to say no to a youth. In addition to the benefits afforded the prospects, the rewards to the teenager are innumerable. Many times I have seen the joy in their eyes as they came running to me: "I just set up a Bible study with Mrs. Holder down the street!" Recreational activities just don't produce that gleam, so here's another thing: Teens who learn to be soul winners don't usually grow up to be backsliders.

- If you were to explain to God that you do not know enough to teach others, what do you suppose His answer would be? What are you doing to prepare yourself?

- Find someone who has done door-to-door work successfully and get five helpful actions for good results. Share them with your class.

## Bible Study Gathering

Have personal evangelism parties. Perhaps "parties" is not the right word, but it expresses the idea. We have every other kind of party—parties to sell everything from brushes and cleaners to jewelry. Why not invite your friends to a gathering to sell the gospel?

Teen girls have used the party method effectively to teach their classmates. I have been invited many times to share their joys and anticipations. It is amazing how mature they can be in planning refreshments to show hospitality to their guests. I have also shared their heartache when some of the invited ones did not show. How I wished I could have borne that sorrow and relieved them of the burden, but that is part of growing up. The important thing is to try.

> Only the Word of God can convert.

New converts may be taught in formal classes or privately using DVDs or other materials. Why not invite a new Christian into your home, along with four or five other women in her general age category and with similar interests? In addition to teaching a new convert, you are helping her become better acquainted with fellow Christians. We must stop thinking that teaching ends when the person is baptized. That is only the beginning. If more people were more interested in more teaching for new converts, more would remain faithful to the Lord.

Many elderly in your community would be delighted to have you teach a Bible class in their home. True, loneliness might be their initial motive, but what an excellent opportunity to teach them the truth. Familiarize yourself with available resources from your congregation, or order your own through a reliable source such as World Video Bible School. Be on the lookout for visuals of Joseph, of Moses, of Christ—anything to grab attention so you can teach the gospel.

Don't try to be the judge of who will accept the gospel. Teach it and leave the results to God. It is amazing how the Word of God can change the life of the sinner. Look at what happened to Saul.

Review the parable of the soil and the sower (Matthew 13:1–9, 18–23).

What is the seed?

What was the sower's primary concern?

How did the soil affect the sower's work?

What if the good soil never met the sower?

Tell another Christian about your prospect, but don't ask anyone else to do your work if you can do it. If, however, you are unable to reach a person with the gospel, recommend that prospect to another teacher. The leaders of the church are always looking for someone who is willing to study. You can pave the way by being a good example and doing good deeds. Only the Word of God can convert, but going out of your way to be nice to someone may make the difference in their willingness to listen to or their refusal to hear God's Word.

Class Activity: Each class member gets a small card and answers these two questions:

1. With how many people have you personally studied the Bible?

2. How many of those studies resulted in conversion?

No names are to be signed. The teacher collects the cards and reports the averages in both categories.

## CONCLUSION

You might at first teach others out of a sense of duty, but soon you will find joy. Once you have had a part in leading a soul to Christ, you will never be the same. Never again will you feel at peace with yourself unless you are actively trying to win someone to Christ. It can become an obsession, but what a wonderful obsession!

Kim

CHAPTER 9

# TEACHING THE YOUNGER WOMEN

*Aged women . . . teach the young women.*

**—Titus 2:4 (KJV)**

Every new generation must be taught. The task of teaching the younger women in the church falls heavily upon the shoulders of the older women.

> The older women likewise, that they be reverent in behavior, not slanderers, not given to much wine, teachers of good things—that they admonish the young women to love their husbands, to love their children, to be discreet, chaste, homemakers, good, obedient to their own husbands, that the word of God may not be blasphemed (Titus 2:3–5).

It is certainly in keeping with the thoughts of this passage to say that older women should be examples and teachers of younger women in every phase of the Christian woman's work. A man simply cannot teach a woman how to do God's work as well as another woman can.

Here is another observation: You don't have to be eighty years old to teach younger women. A mature Christian who has proven herself faithful can be an excellent teacher inside or outside the classroom.

Teaching does not have to be done in a formal classroom setting. Much can and should be done by example and encouragement in the normal course of everyday activities.

Any faithful older Christian woman can find ways of strengthening younger women. If the elders approve, why not, on your own initiative, lead the younger women, including teenage girls, in some of the works listed below? They will gladly participate if you will take the trouble to guide them. They are not likely to be active, mature workers unless they catch a glimpse of the joy that comes through serving. that's where we older women come in.

Teaching does not have to be done in a formal classroom setting.

Once or twice a month, invite teen girls into your home to join you in some regular Christian activity. Refreshments can be simple—or not at all. If your working hours involve meal time, let each girl bring her own sandwich.

The suggestions listed below are not new but they work. You can probably add many more to the list.

## Practical Suggestions

1. *Cookies and candy for the sick and shut-ins*—The size of your kitchen and your innate patience will determine whether the baking is done at your house or at one of the girls' houses. If at the girls' houses, then the packages can be prepared at your house. Look around for suitable containers. Colored paper plates are attractive, yet inexpensive. Many fruits and vegetables are sold in various types of plastic trays. Cover coffee cans and shortening cans with adhesive-backed paper. Frozen juice cans may also be covered and used. Creatively

add bits of lace and trimming to them, and you can produce a real keepsake.

Wrap the little packages with clear plastic wrap and add a festive touch by then wrapping them in nylon net. It's inexpensive and colorful.

Don't neglect the elderly and shut-ins in your own congregation and neighborhood. A person doesn't have to be bedfast to enjoy being remembered. Most nursing homes appreciate such thoughtful gestures by young people. Check with the administration before you distribute baked goods. Perhaps you will be furnished a list of approved patients to receive the cookies and candies since some patients are on restricted diets. Many groups remember the nursing homes during special seasons but forget them during normal times. Surprises on regular humdrum days can really boost morale.

2. *Fruit trays for the sick and shut-ins*—Using the principles mentioned above, substitute fruit for cookies and candy and please the elderly and shut-ins. Sometimes fruits are more suitable than baked sweets.

3. *Cards for shut-ins and the sick*—A card from Hallmark is nice, but one you make says you really care. With a little imagination your group can make attractive cards for pennies.

    - Cut and fold a sheet of colored paper to a suitable size.

    - Let some of the girls compose a verse and print it on the card with a fine-tip felt marker.

    - Or print verses on colored paper in pretty fonts from the computer.

    - Save small desk calendar sheets with pithy sayings or scriptures. Often the photos are striking.

- Get several of your friends to save lace and bits of trimming from their sewing, and see what a difference it makes when they are glued on the cards with rubber cement.

- Keep your eyes open for dress material decorated with small figures of animals or flowers. When those figures are cut out and glued on the card, its appearance takes on a 3-D effect. If the animal is a deer, for example, you may begin the verse by saying, "You're such a deer . . ."

- Some of the girls may want to design their cards with the computer.

  These cards may be mailed directly to the recipients or placed in the packages of candy and fruit.

4. *Cards for absentees in children's classes*—Bible teachers of small children will gladly welcome something different to send to their little absentees. Collect old picture books from parents whose children have outgrown them, and let the girls cut out the pictures. A nursery rhyme figure glued on a postcard with the words, "We missed you last Sunday," will mean more to a child than a commercial card will. Your girls may either supply these cards to the teachers or obtain a list of absentees and mail personally.

5. *Small gifts for sick absentees*—Every sick child likes to be remembered, especially with a package he can unwrap. Frozen juice cans covered with adhesive backed paper, decorated with rick-rack and filled with candy will make any child's eyes light up. Glue attractive pictures to cardboard and cut them to make a puzzle.

   The suggestions mentioned under number 7 below, "Gifts for Children in Hospitals," are also applicable here. Obtain the names of sick children from their Bible class teachers. And remember that mumps and measles are real sicknesses to a child, and all children like to be noticed.

6. *Tray favors for the hospitals*—Delightful tray favors may be made at practically no cost. Fold a square of medium weight paper (approximately three inches by three inches) in the middle, and glue a flower sticker or a bit of trimming from your sewing box on the front and print a suitable Bible verse. Write the name of the congregation on the back. The tiny patients in children's hospitals love these favors. Instead of a flower, cut figures from discarded picture books, mount them on heavy paper, and glue the lower half to the base of the favor. On the front write, "Get Well Soon / from the church." Attach a goodie, such as a small lollipops. Incidentally, it is good to check with hospital officials before planning such an activity.

7. *Gifts for needy children in hospitals*—When children from middle-class and well-to-do homes are in the hospital, they are usually showered with visits and gifts. But many children never receive a single remembrance. By using their hands, young girls may brighten the day of a less fortunate child. Look through books on handwork for ideas. Use your imagination.

8. *Fuzzy animals*—Cut animals from cardboard, using pictures from coloring books as patterns, and cover them with fuzzy cloth. Make eyes, noses, and mouths of felt, and glue them on. By making the animals double (joined at the head), they will stand up. Dogs, cats, and donkeys are good subjects.

9. *Puppets*—Any child who must lie flat on his back loves a puppet. Puppets may be made from small brown paper sacks with faces pasted on, or they may be sewn from terry cloth. The heads of a father, a mother, and children may be glued to rings of paper large enough to fit the child's fingers. A child may amuse himself for hours with a family of puppets.

10. *Sock faces*—Buy stretch socks in children's sizes, and create a face on the toe (facing the child) using yarn, embroidery thread, and bits of felt.

11. *Dolls*—All sorts of dolls may be made from scraps of material, even clothespin dolls. Something soft to hold will thrill a little girl. An ideal doll for a very young child may be made from a powder puff. Just glue felt on it for the facial features or make them with a felt-tip marker.

12. *Bulletin boards*—Most adults are too busy to fix the bulletin boards at the church building and will welcome a little help from the teen girls. Give the girls a little guidance and instruction, and you may be surprised at their ability. They may also keep a supply of letters cut out for others to use.

13. *Teaching aids*—What teacher has enough time to prepare all the aids she would like to use in her class? In this area the younger women can perform a real service, either by making visual aids for a specific lesson for a teacher or by adding to the supply in the audio-visual aids room. They may cut flannel-graph figures, paint flannel background scenes, make puppets, or make Bible-time dolls. Ask the person in charge what sort of work needs to be done. Your offer of assistance will be welcomed.

14. *Posters*—Every congregation has some program that needs publicizing: a gospel meeting, vacation Bible school, special classes for teens. Get the young girls together for a poster-making session. An opaque projector is a valuable aid, but it is not necessary. The posters may be placed on local church bulletin boards—home and neighboring—and in business establishments. People will usually notice a neat, clever, home-made poster more readily than a commercially printed one.

15. *Instruction in teaching methods*—Why not invite the girls to your home for a teacher training course? Give them some practical tips on developing Bible class presentations using different styles and teaching. Help them to make visual aids and let them practice weaving them into the lesson as they present it.

16. *Office work*—Some congregations do not have a secretary to care for all the details of the office, and the elders may welcome help from the teenagers to perform routine tasks, such as folding and addressing bulletins. Check with the person responsible for those tasks and offer to guide the girls in lending a helping hand.

17. *Building cleaning*—A church building, just like a home, periodically needs deep cleaning. Properly supervised, a group of teens can wash a lot of windows and polish many floors. As with all the other suggestions, check with the proper authority to see if your services are needed.

> Whatever you do . . . do all in the name of the Lord Jesus (Colossians 3:17).

18. *Food for the bereaved and sick*—Teenage girls are usually overlooked in this phase of the church's work, but they are capable of fixing some delicious dishes. Often they lack transportation, which you may provide. When a need arises for a home-cooked meal, call several young girls to prepare dishes. Then take them to distribute their food. Giving them an opportunity to serve will lead them to appreciate the true joy of Christianity. Don't overlook newcomers in the community. Take a couple of girls with you as you welcome new families with something fresh from your oven.

19. *Visits to the sick and elderly*—Every faithful Christian woman visits the sick and elderly, either at a private home or in a nursing home. The next time you go, invite one or two teenage girls to go with you. Encourage your friends to do the same. It won't be long until you will have a waiting list.

20. *Dinner for the visiting preacher*—Girls don't have to wait until they are adults to show hospitality. Invite a visiting preacher to your home for a meal, and arrange for a few teens to bring special dishes. They will enjoy the opportunity to prepare something for the visitor and will also benefit from the companionship.

21. *Attendance at meetings*—Young people can learn to put spiritual matters first and enjoy doing so if you will show them how. Youth meetings and regular gospel meetings are much more enjoyable if you can go in a group. Encourage your friends to furnish transportation also, and support sister congregations in their efforts. On the way home, it's nice to stop by a restaurant or your house for a snack.

22. *Fellowship in your home*—It's a shame that more parents don't encourage their children to invite friends into their homes. Young people need to be together in wholesome association. Use your home for singing, discussion groups, progressive dinners, and spend-the-night parties.

23. *Door-to-door work*—Teens usually have better results than adults in going from door to door searching for people to take correspondence courses or to engage in a home Bible study. People hate to refuse a young person who is interested in something so worthwhile and wholesome. It is usually best if an adult does the follow-up work in teaching, but teens have the energy to canvass an entire town in search of prospects. The work should be initiated by the elders, but offer your services in transporting the teens.

24. *Mission meetings*—If you want to help young people discover the real purpose of their existence, accompany them on a mission meeting. The elders usually select a mission point in need of assistance in canvassing its town for prospects. The young people work hard, but there is also a lot of physical labor for the adults who accompany them. You may stay in motels or in the homes of the church members, but you will achieve a greater closeness if you can camp together in some nearby area. You will be physically exhausted after helping cook breakfast for forty each morning and acting as a second mother for about thirty youngsters, but you will never forget the sounds of their singing and devotionals around the campfire. And you will always remember the radiance in their eyes as they run to tell you of a home Bible study they have just set up. It's worth every bit of the work.

25. *Evangelism meetings for teens*—Young people can be quite zealous in their desire to convert others. Why not offer your home to them so they can invite their friends over to see a DVD on becoming a Christian? Or why not urge them to have Bible studies with friends in their own homes. Stand beside them when their friends turn them down. Encourage them to keep on trying.

26. *Chores to help widows*—We take so many things for granted, one of them being the ability to work. Some in every congregation need help with special cleaning jobs. Many widows lack the know-how to do the tasks their husbands once performed. Teenagers can wash walls, clean storm windows, mow grass, and do countless other chores, if they have a little guidance. Recently I visited a widow who proudly showed me her clean kitchen walls—washed by a teenage boy in the congregation. He never mentioned it to anyone.

27. *Care for small children*—Many mothers of small children would like to be involved in a visitation program but do not have the resources to hire babysitters. Urge the young girls to offer their services free of charge, twice each month, so those mothers can make hospital visits and attend to other pressing matters. If the mothers are hesitant to leave their children in the care of teenagers, offer to let the teenagers keep the youngsters in your home so you can keep an eye on them.

28. *Sew for the needy*—Many teens are excellent seamstresses. Encourage the girls to sew for needy children. Elders should be using the talents of young girls in the organized benevolence program of the church.

29. *Gifts for needy families*—Teenagers often get together for a holiday party and exchange comical gifts. Instead of bringing a general gift for someone at the party, encourage them to bring toys for less fortunate children. Perhaps you could get a hint list from the children's mothers.

*Tell me and I forget, teach me and I may remember, involve me and I learn.*

—Benjamin Franklin

*Not everyone who says to Me, "Lord, Lord," shall enter the kingdom of heaven, but he who does the will of My Father in heaven* (Matthew 7:21).

—Jesus

Circle the word that best depicts the common thread of the quotes above:

Talk Activity Heaven

## Conclusion

You can add many more suggestions to the list for teaching by example. The whole idea is to help young girls see Christianity as a way of life. If they learn at an early age to look for work to do, they will probably never become adults who complain because the elders don't give them any assignments.

Putting young women to work in the Lord's kingdom at an early age is the best thing you can do for them. But we often get the cart before the horse. We frantically run around trying to plan socials to pamper our young people and keep them entertained.

Put young women to work; don't just entertain them.

Teenagers have a basic need to be together in wholesome recreation, but entertainment for the sake of entertainment can be boring. Like happiness, fellowship is something we discover unexpectedly. Have you ever heard of the word *serendipity*? It means a fortunate happenstance or pleasant surprise. Happiness is quite evasive. Henry David Thoreau said, "Happiness is like a butterfly; the more you chase it, the more it will elude you, but if you turn your attention to other things, it will come and sit softly on your shoulder." Happiness and fellowship are by-products. We engage in useful and worthwhile activities and suddenly realize that we are extremely happy. Never hesitate to ask someone to do something in the Lord's kingdom. You are doing the person a favor.

CHAPTER 10

# BEING A CHRISTIAN MOTHER

*Her children rise up and call her blessed.*

**—Proverbs 31:28**

Do you remember the first time you held each of your children in your arms? It's an indescribable feeling—a mixture of love, wonder, awe, and fear. Our lips could utter the same words that were spoken of John the Baptist: "What kind of child will this be?" (Luke 1:66).

The child is not yours. God has loaned him to you for a few years for the purpose of molding and training him. For better or for worse your mark will be indelibly stamped on this being for life. His eternal destination may depend upon the teaching you implant in his mind. What a fearsome responsibility!

A group of tourists were gazing at a sculptured image of Abraham Lincoln. An aspiring student of art at a nearby university remarked, "Wouldn't it be wonderful to be the artist who created this masterpiece?" An elderly woman responded: "I'd much rather be the mother who trained the man whose likeness it bears."

## What the Scriptures Say

Proverbs 22:6 is perhaps the most familiar passage concerning the rearing of children: "Train up a child in the way he should go, and when he is old he will not depart from it." It would be nice if we had a step-by-step set of rules which, when followed, would guarantee a perfect child. But the Scriptures give the principles, and it's up to us to apply them.

One thing is certain: the proper training of a child cannot be done without discipline. Notice these passages:

1. Proverbs 29:15—"The rod and rebuke give wisdom, but a child left to himself brings shame to his mother."
2. Proverbs 23:13–14—"Do not withhold correction from a child, for if you beat him with a rod, he will not die. You shall beat him with a rod, and deliver his soul from hell."
3. Proverbs 19:18—"Chasten your son while there is hope, and do not set your heart on his destruction."
4. Proverbs 13:24—"He who spares his rod hates his son, but he who loves him disciplines him promptly."

What does Proverbs 29:15 say regarding a child left to himself? In what sense might this scripture address the modern trend of entrusting the care of our children to someone outside the family.

Read Proverbs 23:13–14 and Proverbs 19:18. Summarize God's attitude toward physical punishment.

## Tried and Tested Principles

The task of training children would be greatly simplified if childrearing were like making a cake. If only we could be told the necessary ingredients, the amounts, and the proper mixing procedures, we could produce an ideal child. But even cakes sometime fail and, after all, a child is not a cake. And there are no infallible rules because each individual is different. We may become discouraged and frustrated when our efforts have failed. Sometimes we are tempted to envy the woman of Proverbs 31, of whom it is said: "Her children rise up and call her blessed." At times it seems as if all our children ever do is rise up and call us! In infancy they usually rise up and call us around two in the morning. As the years go by, the wail of the baby changes to the moaning of the teenager: "Mother, where did you put my blue skirt? I must have it for tonight."

As hopeless as the situation may seem in moments of despair, there are some principles that will produce the desired results if they are followed faithfully.

1. *Be the kind of person you should be.* This principle is more important than all the child-rearing books ever written. It is hypocritical to tell a child to do one thing and then take an opposite course of action. Attitudes are caught, not taught. Children sense what is

really important to you. Much of the youthful rebellion is caused by a discrepancy in what parents teach and what they do. Children who are told to be honest and then see a parent use his influence to get a traffic ticket torn up are really not going to pay very much attention to other parental platitudes.

A child needs a parent, not a buddy.

Mothers who want their daughters to be good homemakers should take a positive attitude toward their own homemaking instead of constantly complaining of its drudgery.

How can parents expect their children to have the right attitude toward God when they don't? Parents moan and wring their hands when their children leave the church, but too often those same children saw their parents allow every flimsy excuse imaginable to keep them from worshiping regularly. If company or a slight headache or bad weather kept them from worship, their children probably concluded that God really did not mean much to them. Even children whose parents worshiped regularly but otherwise showed little love for God may also reach a negative conclusion about religion.

Our discriminating selection of friends teaches our children that associates are important. It is far better than nagging them about running around with the wrong crowd.

How can you conclude that Lois and Eunice were not negative, whining, backsliding, hypocritical women? (2 Timothy 1:5; 3:15).

2. *Accept the child for what he is.* You can't expect a flute to sound like a harp, no matter how hard you try. Although quite different, each instrument has its own useful function. Each child also has a different basic personality. That personality should be developed to its fullest potential within its own limitations. Parents with only one child may fail to realize that no two children are alike. How sad it is when parents try to have their own ambitions fulfilled in the lives of their children. How many warped personalities have developed because mothers and daddies have forced their children into occupations for which they were unsuited. Why should a child be made to feel inadequate simply because he has no desire to participate in sports? Help the child develop his talents to the fullest, but don't force him into areas in which he has no desire or ability.

3. *Be a loving parent.* Most children already have enough buddies. A child really needs a parent—a trusted adult, not someone his own age. A mother cannot be happy living in a child's world. For her emotional well-being, she must have adult friends and adult activities. Parents who try to be buddies to their children are usually too permissive. Children need adult examples to emulate.

4. *Demonstrate love through consistent discipline.* The easiest course is usually the line of least resistance. It is much more trouble to discipline children than to allow them to do as they please. Childhood is a time of preparation for life in the adult world, and the adult world has no place for spoiled brats. If we want our children to be loved and accepted as adults, we must teach them acceptable behavior during their formative years.

   Think back over the scriptures mentioned earlier. Most of them dealt with discipline. The Israelites placed such importance on discipline that unruly children were to be stoned (Deuteronomy

21:18–21). Eli was condemned because he failed to restrain his disrespectful sons, Hophni and Phinehas (1 Samuel 3:13).

There is security in rules of conduct. Complete freedom can be quite frustrating. No child really wants it. Bad behavior is often a cry for help, a subconscious pleading for guidelines. The child wants to know how far he can go. He will test us to see if we will compromise our position, but secretly he doesn't want us to.

Mothers and daddies should be united on their rules of conduct. Any differences should be settled in private so the child sees a united front.

Parents should be consistent and fair. If a child is forbidden to engage in a certain activity one day but gets by with it the next day, he will become so confused that he really won't know what to do. What a rude awakening is in store for him in the adult world when he learns that rules don't change just because he throws a tantrum.

Try to administer corrective discipline in love, not anger. (This is easier said than done.) Don't take advantage of your child just because you are bigger than he is.

5. *Make the child feel loved and accepted.* If a child feels wanted and loved at home, he has a priceless qualification for conquering the world. We disapprove of our children's wrong deeds, but we always love them. Too many parents show their love only through material gifts—a poor substitute for love.

6. *Realize you are only human.* Don't expect to be perfect, because you won't be. Just as you love your children in spite of all their faults, can you not expect the same love from them? Some days you will be cross and irritable when their conduct does not justify that kind of behavior. Before they go to sleep that night, don't be too proud to tell them that you did wrong, and ask their forgiveness. In addition to the benefits you receive, you will be teaching them a valuable

principle for good mental health: you don't have to be perfect to be loved.

- Choose a Bible character who depicts a great quality of motherhood. Write your choice below, supported with scripture.

- What are the harmful effects of forcing a child into hobbies or a profession in which he has no interest or aptitude? Discuss the principle of accepting a child for what he is in light of Proverbs 22:6. Research the word *way* in that text.

## THE PATIENCE TO DO WHAT WE SHOULD

Most Christian mothers know what principles they should apply in rearing children, but they lack the patience to put them into practice. We sometimes pray for patience and expect an immediate answer in an almost miraculous form. Romans 5:3 tells how God answers such petitions: "And not only that, but we also glory in tribulations, knowing that tribulation produces perseverance." We ask for patience but fail to realize that all the petty annoyances involved in rearing small children are the answers to our prayers.

Any young mother knows what I am talking about, and the older ones can well remember the mounds of laundry, the countless nights of interrupted sleep, a toddler's endless curiosity, the times when it seems as if the bronchitis will never break up, the endless cups of milk mopped from the floor, the sibling arguments you have refereed, the services you attended without hearing a word the preacher said, and the utter fatigue at the end of each day. All these petty tribulations serve a purpose. They mold us into more patient mothers. Have you ever wondered why your children's childish traits do not bother their grandmother nearly as much as they bother you? Have you considered that some of your childish escapades might have been the tribulation that wrought the patience in her?

> When all kinds of trials and temptations crowd into your lives, my brothers, don't resent them as intruders, but welcome them as friends! Realize that they come to test your faith and to produce in you the quality of endurance. But let the process go on until that endurance is fully developed, and you will find you have become men of mature character with the right sort of independence. And if, in the process, any of you does not know how to meet any particular problem, he has only to ask God—who gives generously to all men without making them feel foolish or guilty—and he may be quite sure that the necessary wisdom will be given him (James 1:2–5 J. B. PHILLIPS TRANSLATION).

What impresses you about this passage? How does it relate to motherhood?

## Teenage Years

Teen years are the most difficult for child-rearing. They form a bridge between childhood and adulthood. It is a time of great change and transition. Most teens make the adjustment very well. It is the parents who have the most difficulty. Let's look at points to consider that will help parents cross this bridge confidently.

1. *Rebellion.* A teen is naturally somewhat rebellious against his parents. If children were to continue idolizing and clinging to their mothers, they could never be on their own. You wouldn't want your daughter to be still at home at age forty, would you? So don't take your teenager's seeming rejection and personal criticism of you personally, so long as it is not done disrespectfully. It is only a part of growing up.

2. *Boundaries.* A teen still needs clearly defined limits. Rebellion is characteristic, but teenagers don't want complete freedom. They still need the security of rules of conduct. A seventeen-year-old high school senior recently wrote a columnist regarding her mother. In her letter she complained because her mother didn't make her do anything. She even felt jealous of her friends because their mothers gave them orders.

   Another teen wrote to stress the importance of restrictions to teenagers. She told of a freshman scientist who watched a butterfly struggle to get out of its cocoon. The scientist, in an attempt to aid the creature, made tiny slits in the cocoon. That worked beautifully for a quick and easy release, but the butterfly's abdomen was swollen and its wings were shriveled.

Trials? Welcome them as friends.

The struggle would have pushed the fluid from the abdomen into the wings. So the creature, aided by the "scientist," crawled around for a while and then died.

The restrictions we place on our children should be reasonable and fair, but they should be enforced with consistency if we really love our teenagers and want them to grow into responsible adults.

- What sentence did God pronounce on unruly Israelite children? (Deuteronomy 21:18–21).

- Consider the children in your acquaintance. Select one of the best and one of the worst. Analyze the homelife and training of each.

## Four Areas of Growth

We are not being good mothers unless we help our children develop in four important areas. Christ "increased in wisdom and stature, and in favor with God and men" (Luke 2:52).

1. *Wisdom*—A child receives most of his academic training in school, but we can provide a suitable climate for its cultivation. We are depriving our children of much pleasure in life if we fail to introduce them to great literature, to cultivate a love for travel, to give them an opportunity to love good music, to set a proper example

in speech and vocabulary, and to exercise their brains in the art of thinking and reasoning.

2. *Stature*—Most of our time is devoted to the care of our children's physical bodies: meal preparation, sewing, washing and ironing, and housecleaning. Those tasks may be menial and commonplace, but someone has to do them. It makes a difference when such activities are done in love.

3. *In favor with God*—Our child's spiritual growth should be more important than any other phase of his maturation. From the time he is a baby we should talk to him about God. Even when he is only a baby, he learns, through being taken to worship, that the church is important. In family devotionals we shape his life by talking about the Lord's teaching and His example. We cannot begin to train him too soon.

4. *In favor with man*—We want our children to grow in the social graces. Our loving discipline during their childhood teaches them how they must behave if they are to live at peace with others. In addition to discipline, we teach our children how to get along with others by encouraging them to entertain their friends in our homes.

When a child has grown properly in those four areas, he will naturally experience growth in a fifth area—emotional development. A person who is well adjusted intellectually, physically, spiritually, and socially will be blessed with an unexpected by-product—emotional adjustment. Don't ask for happiness for your children. Teach them to be the kind of persons they should be, and they will be happy.

CHAPTER 11

# BEING A CHRISTIAN WIFE

*Wives, submit to your own husbands, as to the Lord.*

**—Ephesians 5:22**

"I take thee to be my wedded husband, to have and to hold from this day forward—for better, for worse; for richer, for poorer; in sickness and in health; to love and to cherish; till death do us part."

Few couples really have any idea what they are promising as they repeat their marriage vows. Their starry-eyed bliss makes it seem as if nothing could ever happen to their joyful union. Divorce statistics, even within the church, prove otherwise. Every Christian woman should be vitally interested in doing everything possible to be a wife pleasing to God.

## From the Beginning

God was well pleased with all His creation except one. Of everything else He was able to say it was good. Bachelor Adam was the problem, so God said, "It is not good that man should be alone" (Genesis 2:18). To fulfill Adam's need for physical, spiritual, social, and emotional companionship, woman was created as a helper suitable for man. By the side of a man, woman finds her greatest contentment and sense of accomplishment. It was for this purpose that she was created.

Only when a woman marries a Christian can the marital union begin to approach its potential happiness. Too many marriages are like a line segment with husband and wife representing the end points. When a disagreement arises, the only direction in which they can travel is apart. A Christian marriage, however, assumes the shape of a triangle with God at the apex and husband and wife at the remaining vertices. When a disagreement arises, as it surely will, Christian mates may be drawn closer as they approach the throne of God on bended knees with their problems instead of being pulled away from each other.

*Therefore what God has joined together, let not man separate* (Mark 10:9). Read this verse in context and comment on how it supports the idea of a Christian marriage as a triangle.

## What the Scriptures Say

The husband-wife relationship is more important than all other earthly relationships.

> Therefore a man shall leave his father and mother and be joined to his wife, and they shall become one flesh (Genesis 2:24).

Husbands and wives who are not mature enough to leave their parents and gladly follow their mates to the ends of the earth, if necessary, are not ready for marriage. Leaving father and mother implies more than physical distances. It also means leaving them emotionally, that the newlyweds stand on their own two feet and do not run to their parents when little spats occur in marriage.

God intended only one mate at a time (Matthew 5:31–32; 19:3–12; Luke 16:18). From the beginning He planned for marriage to be monogamous. Because of the hardness of the hearts of the Israelites, Moses allowed divorce. But it displeased God even then. Only death can honorably end the marriage contract (Romans 7:1–3). A partner's unfaithfulness may also sever the ties, but that could never be considered honorable.

> A wife is bound by law as long as her husband lives; but if her husband dies, she is at liberty to be married to whom she wishes, only in the Lord (1 Corinthians 7:39).

Marriage is honorable. Hebrews 13:4 specifically says, "Marriage is honorable among all, and the bed undefiled; but fornicators and adulterers God will judge. Also Proverbs 18:22 says, "He who finds a wife finds a good thing, and obtains favor from the Lord." And God condemned false teachers who forbade Christians to marry (1 Timothy 4:1–3).

## Purposes

One purpose of marriage is the lawful and honorable fulfillment of fleshly desires. Paul shares his inspiration concerning marriage with specific instructions concerning the manner in which a husband and wife should treat one another's bodies:

Oneness is not complete until both function as a single unit socially and emotionally.

> Nevertheless, because of sexual immorality, let each man have his own wife, and let each woman have her own husband (cf. 1 Corinthians 7:2).

Physical union is implied when God speaks of husband and wife becoming one flesh (Genesis 2:24; 1 Corinthians 6:16; Matthew 19:5–6), but oneness is not complete until both function as a single unit socially and emotionally.

Children should be desired as a result of this union. First Timothy 5:14 says, "Therefore I desire that the younger widows marry, bear children, manage the house, give no opportunity to the adversary to speak reproachfully."

The wife is in subjection to her husband. As the result of the first sin in the Garden of Eden, Eve and all wives who came after her were placed under the rule of their husbands. "Your desire shall be for your husband, and he shall rule over you" (Genesis 3:16). In Titus 2:5 the younger women are taught to be "obedient to their own husbands, that the word of God may not be blasphemed." Direct commands are given by Peter and Paul:

- *Wives, likewise, be submissive to your own husbands* (1 Peter 3:1).
- *Wives, submit to your own husbands, as to the Lord* (Ephesians 5:22).

Like it or not, there it is in black and white. A woman who marries the right kind of man should not resent being under his authority because he will love, cherish, and honor her as Christ does the church (Ephesians 5:23–25). She will truly reign as queen. A woman who marries a man who treats her as if she were a slave is still under his subjection. She should have been more selective in her choice of a lifelong companion. (Review chapter 1 to see God's reasons for this relationship.)

How can older married women stress to single women the seriousness of willingly placing herself in submission to the man she chooses as a husband?

## Woman's Home

A woman's domain is her home. God decreed that Adam should provide the physical necessities for his family (Genesis 3:17–19). It is the husband's place to earn a living for the family, if he is physically able. Although the man is head of his house, day-to-day operational matters are delegated to the wife. In 1 Timothy 5:14 the younger women are told to "manage the house." Paul reinforced this command when he told Titus that older women should teach younger women "to be discreet, chaste, homemakers" (Titus 2:5). The Proverbs 31 woman is a paragon of a wife who oversees the caring of her family with the utmost efficiency.

Some women have the ability to run a home smoothly and still have many outside interests. Each woman must judge her abilities in this respect. Her home is her first concern. As stated before, when a woman seeks gainful employment for her fulfillment or busies herself with community and civic interests that rob her of necessary time needed for the welfare of her family, she is wrong. And she adds to the wrong when she expects her husband to assume her duties, whether it be mopping the floors or constantly caring for the children. The husband who allows his wife to domesticate him is just as guilty.

> It is wrong when she expects her husband to assume her duties, whether it be mopping floors or constant child care.

Love is involved in marriage. Even when women were treated as chattel and marriages were frequently arranged by parents, love was an essential part of marriage. The aged women in the early church were to teach the younger women to "love their husbands" (Titus 2:4). Husbands are also told to "love your wives, just as Christ also loved the church and gave Himself for her" (Ephesians 5:25). We use *love* to express our likeness for everything from chocolate pie to a new dress. A fuller treatment of the meaning of love will be considered later in this discussion.

Explain why Titus 2:4 instructs older women to teach the younger ones to love their husbands. If they are married, why shouldn't they already love their husbands? What are your suggestions for exactly how to teach this love?

## Oneness in Marriage

In the beginning God decreed that man and woman should become one flesh (Genesis 2:24). Christ repeated these words when He was discussing the question of divorce with the Pharisees: "So then, they are no longer two but one flesh" (Matthew 19:6). Paul refers to the union of a man and a woman as one flesh (1 Corinthians 6:16).

A husband and wife should function as one in many areas of life: physical, emotional, spiritual, social. No longer are they two separate individuals, each going a separate way. The partner's needs should be considered before making any decision so the two may act as one.

Too many couples, however, seem to have the wrong concept of oneness in marriage. Some view marriage as a rope in which the two separate parts are intertwined to make one whole, abandoning all personal identity. A wife may feel chagrined if the husband has any hobbies or activities that do not include her. A "rope" marriage may strangle the love that bonds the relationship.

An ideal marriage may be compared to a railroad track. Both rails have the same goal. They travel to the same destination side by side but not intertwined. A railroad track appears as a single unit, but it is made up of two rails kept parallel by myriads of crossties. It is a happy, well-adjusted husband and wife who realize that their partner must be allowed some personal freedom in their union. No two people are alike. Each of us comes from a different environment with different likes and dislikes, different strengths and weaknesses. Of course, your husband is different from you. Wouldn't you hate to spend the rest of your life with a person exactly like yourself?

> A clinging wife is a parasite.

We subconsciously seek a mate who will complement our personalities. We want someone who is strong in areas in which we are weak. That is the reason a loquacious wife seeks a taciturn husband. After all, in a marriage of two talkative people, who listens? Naturally your husband has hobbies in which you have no interest. He is not too absorbed in your sewing or crafts either. How would you feel if he threw a temper tantrum every time you wanted to sew because he cannot engage in that activity with you? In a truly happy marriage the partners share major goals, but their minor preferences have enough variety and spice to make the marriage interesting. As long as you and your husband want the same things out of life as your ultimate goals—your service to God, your outlook on life—don't fret if he does not include you in everything he does. A clinging wife is a parasite, not an individual. She has no one to blame but herself if she doesn't have enough backbone to be a separate individual.

Your husband has faults. You do too. If you expect him to make allowances for your weaknesses, is it not fair that you treat him in the same manner? This is one reason marriage is for mature people. They must be able to ascertain before marriage whether or not their own personalities, with their strengths and weaknesses, will be compatible with another set of strengths and weaknesses. Don't marry a man with the idea of reforming him. If you don't like him as he is, don't marry him. Once the marriage vows have been said, you must accept and love him for what he is.

## God's Definition of Love

The love spoken of in 1 Corinthians 13 is broad enough to include all phases of love. For this particular study, however, consider its application to married love.

1. *Love suffers long.* Love does not lose heart. The ability to bear the offenses and injuries of others, more than any other virtue, is necessary when two people are trying to adjust to a relationship. So remember, while you are adjusting to his faults and idiosyncrasies, he is struggling to adjust to yours. All the time you are seething over his failure to pick up his socks, he may be secretly vexed over the way you squeeze toothpaste from the tube. So go ahead and pick up his socks. They are really not that heavy. If your husband has not already been trained to pick up his clothes, it's too late now.

   Instead of looking for faults, search for the good points—he must have had some or you never would have fallen in love with him—and concentrate on those. Elizabeth Barrett Browning expressed this idea so beautifully in these words:

I love you,
Not only for what you
are,
But for what I am
When I am with you.
I love you,
Not only for what
You have made of
yourself,
But for what
You are making of me.
I love you
For the part of me
That you bring out.
I love you
For putting your hand
Into my heaped-up heart
And passing over
All the foolish, weak
things
That you can't help
Dimly seeing there,
And for drawing out
Into the light
All the beautiful
belongings
That no one else had
looked
Quite far enough to find.
I love you because you
Are helping me to make
Of the lumber of my life
Not a tavern
But a temple;
Out of the works
Of my every day
Not a reproach
But a song.

2. *Love is kind.* Does kindness really need a definition? How sad it is when husband and wife treat their dog with more kindness than they show one another. They would not think of treating a stranger with the same rudeness they show within the privacies of their homes. Love does not shout angry words and deliberately try to hurt the feelings of another. We may act that way sometimes, but that is not love. Love shows its kindness by so many little courtesies. It says, "Thank you for going to the trouble of doing that for me." It says,

"I'm sorry. I shouldn't have done that." There are so many ways to say "I love you."

Nagging is not kindness. A very wise writer penned these words: "A continual dripping on a very rainy day and a contentious woman are alike" (Proverbs 27:15). Have you ever listened to the drip, drip, drip of a leaky faucet until you could hardly stand it anymore? Continually nagging our husbands produces the same effect on them. Small wonder they had rather be some place other than home. Make home the warm, inviting place it should be, and the husband will want to be there. If your husband has his own private little hiding place, consider these words: "Better to dwell in a corner of a housetop, than in a house shared with a contentious woman" (Proverbs 21:9).

3. *Love does not envy.* Love trusts. It is not jealous. It is not possessive. The right kind of wife who loves her husband trusts him wherever he is. She is not jealous over his relatives and friends. Her love is big enough to share him with many people. She does not begrudge his hobbies or the money he spends on them. She does not complain of her work while maintaining that his lot in life is easier than hers. She is happy over her husband's trust in her. "The heart of her husband safely trusts her" (Proverbs 31:11).

4. *Love does not parade itself, is not puffed up.* Marriage is no place for the arrogant or conceited person. Humility is essential in this special relationship, for husband and wife must swallow pride and meet one another halfway on controversial situations every day.

   Love is not anxious to impress others with inflated ideas of its own importance. Husbands and wives will naturally have differences, but they should be settled in private. Have you ever witnessed a wife making fun of her husband when in the company of others? That works both ways. How sad it is when a husband boosts his ego at the expense of his wife's feelings by putting her down when they are among friends. While most of us can very gallantly take constructive criticism in private, our feelings are crushed when we are publicly humiliated. Some people cannot feel important until they make someone else seem less important. A boastful person has no place in marriage or in the Lord's kingdom. Our feelings should be as those of Paul: "For when I am weak, then I am strong" (2 Corinthians 12:10).

5. *Love doth not behave rudely.* Love is courteous and polite. It has no place for rudeness. It does not pout, neither is it sullen. A wife will not give her husband the silent treatment for several days before she tells him her grievances. She will not be moody or irritable. We often tell children, "Act your age!" or "Behave yourself!" Many married people need the same advice.

The heart of her husband safely trusts her.

6. *Love does not seek its own.* Love is unselfish in little and big things. Even though a wife may be very tired at the end of a long day spent in caring for her family, her unselfishness causes her to go an extra mile and prepare her husband's favorite dessert just because she loves him. Love is doing something for others. Love does not insist on its own way. A wife who loves her husband will not insist on spending more money on clothes for herself than their budget will allow. She will remember that it boosts her husband's morale when he has something new also. A good wife will not demand so many material things that her husband must take on a second job to pay her bills.

What about the opposite—a marriage in which the husband is too stingy to give the wife any money of her own? Reread the only scriptural reason for divorce in Matthew 5:31–32 and Matthew

19:3–9. Is stinginess mentioned? It may be a miserable existence, but the wife is stuck with her husband for better or for worse. If she wants the "betters" to outnumber the "worses," she should be careful in her selection of a partner for life.

7. *Love is not easily provoked.* Love has an even temper. It is not touchy. Someone has said that you can measure a person's character by the things that make him angry. There are some things in this world important enough to stir up our righteous indignation, but something as trivial as forgetting a birthday just isn't that significant.

It is a wise wife who realizes that she must sometimes act as a lightning rod for her husband's anger when he is frustrated with the world. When he lashes out at her, it does not necessarily mean he is angry with her personally. Things may irritate him in his business world. If he "tells off" his boss, he may lose his job. Instead, he suppresses his emotions until he arrives at the front door. On these days the slightest irritation on the part of his wife may give him the excuse he has been needing to vent his anger. It takes a mature wife to bite her tongue when she has done nothing to justify such a tirade. The temptation to retaliate with similar words is great, but such reaction produces nothing but conflict. Blessed is the woman who can remain calm and give her husband time to cool off.

Love has an even temper.

Many disagreements can be prevented. "A soft answer turns away wrath, but a harsh word stirs up anger" (Proverbs 15:1). Some people have a knack for making others angry. The very tone of their voices can be irritating. Have you ever been so upset with your husband that you have rehearsed all day what you would say to him, only to have your anger melt when he arrived in a pleasant mood? It is difficult to pick a fight with a sweet, lovable person.

Differences will arise and they must be settled. An angry diatribe may relieve your frustrations momentarily, but it rarely solves the original problem. In addition to the unsolved problem, you also must cope with the new problems produced by your angry words. We all say things in anger that we would never utter under normal circumstances. A spoken word can never be recalled, no matter how desperately we try. Each couple should resolve to settle differences as quickly as possible and according to fair rules of disagreement. If you are so angry with your partner that you honestly can't forgive and forget, try talking the problem over with the Lord. Tell Him how upset you are and how many bad feelings are in your heart. He understands. He experienced these feelings when He lived on earth in a human body, but He never sinned. Ask for help in developing a better attitude.

> Love expects the best, not the worst.

8. *Love thinks no evil.* Love expects the best, not the worst in a person. How many marriages have been wrecked because a wife attached some ulterior motive to her husband's every innocent move. In the original Greek text, the verb is an accountant's word for entering items on a ledger. Love does not store up grievances or grudges. It does not keep an account of evil. True love is too big to harbor a wrong. It does not brood over slights or injustices. Some people major in minors. Their chief delight is in remembering the wrongs people have done to them. What a wasted life when there is so much that is good and beautiful!

9. *Love does not rejoice in iniquity but rejoices in the truth.* Love does not gloat over the wickedness of others but is happy when truth or goodness prevails. This characteristic of love is closely connected with the one immediately preceding it. Some wives maliciously take pleasure in their husband's shortcomings. They delight in criticizing him to others. Love is never glad when others go wrong. Your husband has both good and bad in him, and so do you. We usually find what we are looking for. If you want to see his faults, you won't have any trouble. But neither will you have too much difficulty in discovering his good traits.

Why is Philippians 4:8 a practical help in improving the love characteristics 8 and 9?

10. *Love bears all things.* Love knows no limit to its endurance. Most women have only petty grievances to bear. Some must bear real crosses in their marriages. When your husband's behavior seems exasperating at times—too much clutter around his chair, too much sports on TV—talk with a woman who has lived with an alcoholic for twenty years. You will get down on your knees and ask God's forgiveness for your impatience.

11. *Love believes all things.* Love knows no end to its trust. You cannot be with your husband every minute. It is an unwise wife who makes

him account for every minute and every action. If their marital love is what it should be, she has no reason to doubt him.

12. *Love hopes all things.* Love expects the best of its partner. A child behaves better when he knows that his parents expect him to be good and praise him for it. Tell a child over and over he is bad and he will be bad. The same is true of marriage. Even when a marriage has its rough spots, things will usually work out if the partners expect it to. If divorce looms as a possibility in the subconscious mind of each one, problems will be much more difficult to solve.

13. *Love endures all things.* Love never fails. It lasts longer than anything else. The bond between a man and a woman is binding until death. It means fidelity until the end. Love is one of the strongest motivating factors in the world. Christ knew the power of love when He said that all other commandments are dependent on two loves: love for God and love for our fellowman (Matthew 22:35–40). If we truly love God, we will want to obey all His commands. If we love our fellowman, including our husbands, we will somehow find a way to settle our problems.

Choose three of the thirteen characteristics of love that challenge you the most. What steps will you take to improve your love?

## The Seven Stages of the Married Cold

*A husband's reactions to his wife's colds during seven years of marriage.*

**—Source Unknown**

*First year:* "Sugar dumplin'; I'm really worried about my baby girl. You've got a bad sniffle, and there's no telling about these things with all the strep throat going around. I'm putting you in the hospital this afternoon for a general checkup and a good rest.

*Second year:* "Listen, darling, I don't like the sound of that cough, and I've called Doc Miller to rush over here. Now you go to bed like a good girl, just for Poppa."

*Third year*: "Maybe you better lie down, honey. Nothing like a little rest when you feel lousy. I'll bring you something. Have we got any canned soup?"

*Fourth year:* "Now look, dear, be sensible. After you've fed the kids, and got the dishes done, and the floor finished, you better lie down."

*Fifth year:* "Why don't you take a couple of aspirin?"

*Sixth year:* "I wish you'd just gargle or something instead of sitting around barking like a seal all evening."

*Seventh year:* "For Pete's sake, stop sneezing! Are you trying to give me pneumonia?"

## CONCLUSION

Marriage may either be torment on this earth or a taste of heaven. It depends on three factors: the kind of person you are, the kind of person you select for your partner, and how hard you work to make your marriage a success. The right marriage truly becomes sweeter as the years go by.

CHAPTER 12

# ENCOURAGING HER HUSBAND IN GOD'S SERVICE

*Women must likewise be dignified, not malicious gossips, but temperate, faithful in all things.*

**—1 Timothy 3:11 (NASB)**

Are you a help or a hindrance in your husband's service to God? It matters not whether he is an elder, deacon, evangelist, or member without a special work. He serves better if you are by his side encouraging him as a "helper comparable to him" (Genesis 2:18).

## Wives of Elders and Deacons

Specific Qualifications—The Scriptures are very explicit in the qualifications for elders and deacons. First Timothy 3:1–13 and Titus 1:5–9 delineate the characteristics of men whom God expects to hold these offices. Some have maintained that 1 Timothy 3:11 gives the qualifications of the wives of the deacons. "Likewise their wives must be reverent, not slanderers, temperate, faithful in all things." A closer examination of this verse, however, seems to indicate that the women referred to in verse 11 were not the wives of the deacons, but a special group of women who served the early church. Consider these points.

1. The Greek word for wife is *gune* (goo-NAY), which is also translated "woman," depending on the context. "Women" is the only logical translation in this verse, according to a number of Bible scholars.

2. The original language does not use a possessive pronoun. "Their" is inserted by the translators.

3. If these qualifications refer to the wives of the deacons, why were no qualifications given for the wives of those who hold the highest office in the church, the elders?

4. Paul first listed the qualifications for elders (vv. 1–7). He then enumerated several qualifications for deacons (vv. 8–10). Notice how closely these qualifications parallel the qualifications given for this special group of women in verse 11. It seems as if Paul is saying that the deacons must possess certain qualities. Then he breaks into his line of thought to state that women who are servants of the church must also have these same traits. He continues the qualifications of the deacons in verses 12–13.

5. Since the entire chapter deals with officers in the church, the only logical conclusion is that verse 11 refers to special women servants. Phoebe in Romans 16:1 was called a "servant of the church in Cenchrea." The Greek word for servant in this case is the same word that is rendered "deacon" in 1 Timothy 3:8, except it appears here in the feminine gender. Evidently Phoebe was some kind of special servant in the church, a "deaconess."

Although one may not logically claim that the qualifications listed in 1 Timothy 3:11 refer to the wives of the deacons, they are certainly excellent traits of character for any Christian woman, especially the wife whose husband is serving the church. Any Christian woman, and especially the wife of an elder or a deacon, should possess the ability to control her tongue, to be moderate, to be of a serious nature, and to be an example in faithfulness.

## IMPLIED QUALIFICATIONS

After a careful study of the qualifications of elders and deacons, one may well conclude that their wives should possess special traits. Several of the qualifications of elders and deacons are practically impossible without complementary qualifications of their wives.

> Phoebe was a special servant in the church.

1. *She must support her husband's desire to serve as an elder* (1 Timothy 3:1). How can he desire "the position of a bishop" unless his wife is behind him one hundred percent? If she is resentful of his time and effort, he cannot do his best. There will be many evenings tied up with business meetings and many other lonely hours which she must spend because he is doing necessary personal work. Her attitude toward his work can make it a pleasure or a burden.

*This is a faithful saying: If a man* desires *the position of a bishop, he* desires *a good* task (1 Timothy 3:1).

2. *She must help him in extending hospitality* (1 Timothy 3:2). An elder naturally shows hospitality at the church building, but it should extend to his home if his hospitality is to be very effective. Newcomers and weaker members should feel the warmth of the homes of elders and deacons. (See chapter 6.) The shepherds need to know each member of their flock personally. The gift of hospitality makes that a lot easier. How many elders or deacons do you

suppose would ever bake a cake and invite someone over? What an important part the wife plays in helping him fulfill that obligation.

*A ______________ then must be blameless, the husband of one wife, temperate, sober-minded, of good behavior, ________________, able to teach* (1 Timothy 3:2).

3. *She should encourage his studying* (1 Timothy 3:2). An elder must be "able to teach." Teaching requires much hard studying. A wife cannot do her husband's studying for him, but she can certainly make it easier by providing a quiet place and by not making so many demands that he has no time left for studying. Many books will be necessary. So the wife must not act like a martyr over the money he must spend on them.

*A bishop then must be blameless, the husband of one ____________, temperate, sober-minded, of good behavior, hospitable, ____________ to* ________________ (1 Timothy 3:2).

4. *She must not desire more material possessions than her husband can provide.* Both elders and deacons are admonished not to be greedy of filthy lucre (1 Timothy 3:3, 8). Of course even a bachelor may place too much emphasis on material things, but how very difficult it is for a married man to maintain a proper balance between material and spiritual values when his wife is constantly demanding more than he can earn. Her insatiable desires often drive him into taking a second job or spending so many extra hours in his business that he has no time left to do the Lord's special work.

*Not given to wine, not violent, not ______________ for money, but gentle, not quarrelsome, not covetous . . . likewise deacons must be reverent, not double-tongued, not given to much wine, not greedy for* ______________ (1 Timothy 3:3, 8).

5. *She must be in submission to her husband as he rules his house.* Both elders and deacons must rule their own houses well and have their children under proper control (1 Timothy 3:4, 12). A hen-pecked man cannot scripturally qualify for such an office. A man can seldom discipline his children as he should without the full cooperation of his wife. Also, the wife must realize that it is her husband, not she, who does the work of an elder or deacon. She leaves the running of the affairs of the church to her husband.

*One who rules his ______________ house well, having his children in __________________ with all reverence . . . let deacons be the husbands of one wife, __________________ their children and their own _______________ well* (1 Timothy 3:4, 12).

6. *She must do nothing to mar her husband's reputation* (1 Timothy 3:7). "Moreover he must have a good testimony among those who are outside." Since a husband and wife are considered as one (Matthew 19:6), it is practically impossible for an elder to have a good name in the community when his wife has the reputation of being the neighborhood gossip. A good name is truly a treasured possession.

*Moreover he must have a good _________________ among those who are _________________, lest he fall into ________________ and the snare of the devil* (1 Timothy 3:7).

7. *She will not unduly provoke her husband's patience.* An elder must be "gentle, not quarrelsome" (1 Timothy 3:3). He must also be slow to anger (Titus 1:7). It would truly try the patience of Job to live with some women. Their continual faultfinding and nagging would cause anyone to lose patience. Our dispositions can help create a pleasant atmosphere at home, where a proper spiritual attitude can be cultivated.

- *Not given to wine, not violent, not greedy for money, but ______________________, not ______________________, not covetous* (1 Timothy 3:3).

- *For a bishop must be blameless, as a steward of God, not self-willed, not __________ - ____________________, not given to wine, not violent, not greedy for money* (Titus 1:7).

8. *She should be an example of faithfulness.* No one is perfect, but the wife of an elder or deacon should be an example to other women in the congregation. How can an elder admonish others to faithful service when they can point a finger at his wife and ask why he doesn't begin at home. In too many congregations the wives of the other members are far more faithful in the Lord's work than are the wives of the elders and deacons. This can lead only to discontent and justified resentment.

- *And let us ________________ one another in order to ____________ _____ love and good works, not forsaking the ____________________ of ourselves together, as is the manner of some, but ________________ one another* (Hebrews 10:24–25).

9. *She should be master of her tongue.* First, the wives of elders and deacons should realize that their husbands, by the very nature of their work, know confidential things concerning the members of the flock. They should control their feminine impulses to ask about such matters.

   Second, she must learn to control her tongue if her husband decides to talk personal matters over with her. Sometimes he will need someone as a sounding board, not as an advisor. Frequently, a problem may be solved just by thinking out loud. When your husband feels he must talk with you about matters pertaining to his office, relieve him from anxiety by being deserving of his confidence. He needs to know his wife is trustworthy.

He needs to know his wife is trustworthy.

Wives of elders and deacons should not repeat any information that will be detrimental to anyone, whether the information came from their husbands or from some other source. If the slander is conjecture, it certainly should not be repeated. Even known facts should not be passed along if they are harmful or private in nature.

Some knowledge concerning the work of the church may seem too good to keep. Control the impulse and let your husband be the bearer of glad tidings to the congregation. If you tell the good news of confidential business meetings, many members will wonder if you also relate their personal confidences which they have told to the leaders.

*Even so the tongue is a ____________________ member and boasts ________________ things. See how great a forest a ______________ ____________ kindles!* (James 3:5).

10. *Other considerations*—There will be times when an elder will need the presence of his wife as he visits in homes. Her willingness to accompany him and her proper conduct in their home can make his task much easier.

*Do not let your ____________________ be merely outward—arranging the hair, wearing gold, or putting on fine apparel—rather let it be the hidden person of the ______________, with the incorruptible beauty of a ____________ and ____________ spirit, which is very precious in the sight of God. For in this manner, in former times, the holy*

_______________ *who trusted in God also adorned themselves, being submissive to their* _______ *husbands* (1 Peter 3:3–5).

## The Wife of an Evangelist

An evangelist, as in no other line of work, needs a wife who is a suitable helper. In most occupations a man can compartmentalize his life: employment, the Lord's service, family affairs. An evangelist's work is with him twenty-four hours a day; his work is his life. Most wives have only a small interest in their husband's work. They listen to end-of-day talks about people and events connected with his job, but they really aren't part of it.

An evangelist's work is his life.

An evangelist's wife, on the other hand, is very deeply involved in her husband's work. She daily contacts those with whom her husband is working, and she is closely associated with all the events. Scripture is silent concerning her qualifications or duties. Some women are extremely happy in this role. Others are miserable as they dutifully bear a cross.

## Two Loves

If a wife is to be truly contented as she serves beside her evangelist husband, she must have two great loves that are more important than anything else on the face of this earth.

1. *She must love the Lord.* When we love God most, the problems that result from being an evangelist's wife melt into insignificance. If serving God is paramount, more meaningful than possessions or security, then her place at her husband's side is an opportunity for service to God. And if she really loves the Lord, she will love His church.

2. *She must love her husband.* What he enjoys in his work will give pleasure to her. How sad it is when a wife feels jealous of her husband because his service to God comes first in his life. To love a man who is devoting his life to God's work is to love unselfishly with a love that is too deep for possession.

## Fruits of Love

What are the fruits of these two loves? When a wife loves God and her husband more than anything else, certain needed qualifications naturally result.

1. *She realizes the importance of providing a Christian home.* Ministers' families may live in many houses, but they take their homes with them each time they move. Moving every few years, with the breaking of old ties and friendships, plus the trials of becoming adjusted to a new location, can be a rather trying experience. As long as the family acts as a closely knit unit and home is the place it should be, the task becomes much easier. There are many frustrations and tensions which accompany a minister's work. Home should truly be a place of refuge for him—a pleasant, relaxed atmosphere to which he may retreat. When his home life involves just as many problems as his work, a husband can easily break emotionally under the strain.

2. *She will gladly follow him wherever he goes.* The wife of an evangelist will be called upon to display the same maturity as did Ruth when she uttered those beautiful words so long ago: "Wherever you go, I will go" (Ruth 1:16). Not begrudgingly but cheerfully will she leave family and other ties to remain by the side of her husband. Too many times a minister has been restricted in his work because his wife would not move to a different section of the country.

3. *She will use all her talents in the Lord's service.* Evangelists' wives have different abilities for service. Some one-talent wives have been made to feel quite miserable by congregations that expected too much of them, while some five-talent wives have been tempted to use only a small amount of their ability. Because of her position as the wife of the evangelist, many opportunities of service will be opened to her. She should do whatever her hands and her mind find to do as long as she maintains a proper balance in her life. To devote so much time in ministering to the saints that her family and her own health are neglected is wrong. Drudgery and a sense of begrudged duty can drain her energy. The right attitude, resulting in joy in service to others, can produce untapped strength.

4. *She does not pry.* An evangelist knows many confidential matters. His wife respects the responsibility which he must bear and does not try to "pick out" the information. If he needs to discuss matters, just for the sake of thinking through problems, his wife must be so trustworthy that he has no fear that the information will go any further. It must stop with her, no matter how intensely she feels the need to share it. She may provide a sympathetic ear when it is needed, and she must keep her mouth closed.

5. *She respects the needs for her husband to spend time away from her.* He will be engaged in personal work on many lonely evenings, and she must remain home with the children. There will be days at a time when he will be away in meetings. She can either sit at home and mope or she can put the time to good use. Save a few small projects for those special times—reading, in-depth studying, preparing visual aids, sewing, special housecleaning.

6. *She embraces the entire congregation with her love.* If a woman knows she will have difficulty helping to bear the burdens and share the

joys of church members, she should never marry an evangelist. The evangelist's home has to be open in hospitality. She must consider her fellow Christians as part of her family, or her life will be miserable.

Give a life example of a wife who chose to marry a Christian, but failed in her two loves. What are the warning signs of this type failure? How can a Christian woman encourage a weak wife? How do friends sometimes enable a troubled marriage instead of encouraging a couple's happiness?

## The Wife of Any Christian

If your husband does not hold the office of elder, deacon, or evangelist, you can still help him serve God better. Nearly everything that has been mentioned previously is applicable to a degree to you. But here are a few other suggestions.

1. *Be the right kind of spiritual partner.* We all have our spiritual ups and downs. We are sometimes tempted to quit trying, but a spiritual partner makes a life for Christ much easier. When you are at a low spiritual ebb, your husband's strength can carry you through. If you were alone, you might give up. And that works the same for him. The two of you help balance one another.

2. *Discuss your problems with each other and talk them over with the Lord.* It is difficult to remain angry with someone when you can pray together about the matter.

3. *Work with your husband in scheduling family devotionals.* In the average home, there never seems to be enough time for family Bible study. As you work out the daily family schedule, consider putting God first on your list of things to do.

4. *Make your home a haven.* A nagging, contentious wife can cause the best of men to "lose their religion." Home then becomes a battlefield with little spiritual encouragement from anyone. And try as you might, you cannot lift God up in such an environment. Neither your husband nor your children can spiritually survive the fallout that occurs from nagging.

5. *Make preparation for worship as smooth as possible.* Acceptable worship is difficult when family feuds erupt thirty minutes before leaving for worship. Plan the day before. Check buttons, pressing—all those last minute details. The smoothness really depends on you.

6. *Put God first in your budget and live within it.* Many men would like to contribute more to the Lord, but they can't because they have extravagant wives. Along this same line, don't begrudge money he spends on books and other aids that enhance his spirituality.

7. *Don't be overly possessive of your husband.* Your demand for full-time attention is likely to create guilt feelings in him and tempt him to compromise the time he has dedicated to God. Business meetings, personal work, class preparation—all these things are quite time consuming. Make it easier for him to use those hours.

8. *Praise him for the services he performs for the Lord.* Whether he volunteers his carpentry skills or fills the pulpit, let him know how proud

you are of him. If criticism is needed, be certain it is constructive and is given in the right manner.

- Compare the examples of Ananias and Sapphira (Acts 5:1–10) with those of Aquila and Priscilla (Acts 18:24–26).

## Conclusion

You and your husband may be as selfish as Ananias and Sapphira or as devoted as Aquila and Priscilla. The influence of your life can be a determining factor in your husband's eternal destiny, as well as yours. It's an awesome responsibility, isn't it?

CHAPTER 13

# WINNING HER HUSBAND TO CHRIST

*If some do not obey the word, they, without a word, may be won by the conduct of their wives.*

**—1 Peter 3:1**

In an ideal marriage, the husband and wife are both devoted Christians. Only then can they know the full potential of happiness in marriage.

> Do not be unequally yoked together with unbelievers. For what fellowship has righteousness with lawlessness? And what communion has light with darkness? (2 Corinthians 6:14).

The ideal is not always reality. Many Christian women, after a few years of marriage, suddenly awaken to the fact that they selected a non-Christian as a spiritual leader. The instructions given to women in such a predicament nearly two thousand years ago are just as valid today as they were then.

- What scripture supports the claim that the husband is the spiritual leader of the home?

Summarize the Old Testament passages below regarding how God's people were to select marriage partners:

Genesis 6:1–6

Genesis 24:1–4

Genesis 27:46

Deuteronomy 7:3–4

I Kings 11:1–13

Ezra 10:1–14

## Should I Leave Him?

A Christian woman's marriage to an unbeliever, though far from God's wishes, is not an illegal marriage.

> And a woman who has a husband who does not believe, if he is willing to live with her, let her not divorce him. For the unbelieving husband

is sanctified by the wife, and the unbelieving wife is sanctified by the husband; otherwise your children would be unclean, but now they are holy. But if the unbeliever departs, let him depart; a brother or a sister is not under bondage in such cases. But God has called us to peace. For how do you know, O wife, whether you will save your husband? Or how do you know, O husband, whether you will save your wife? (1 Corinthians 7:13–16).

Marriage to an unbeliever is not illegal.

In this passage Paul instructed the newly converted women to remain with their unbelieving husbands if their husbands desired to live with them. A marriage is not illegal just because one is a Christian and the other is not. Neither are their children considered unclean. If the unbelieving husband does not wish to continue living with his Christian wife, however, she had no right to force him to remain. If he dissolves the marriage, she is not responsible for its having ended, because "a brother or a sister is not under bondage in such cases" (1 Corinthians 7:15).

- In 1 Corinthians 7:14 what is meant by "sanctified"?

- A Christian widow is not free to marry just anyone she pleases. Read 1 Corinthians 7:39 and give her limitations.

## Winning without a Word

A woman who has been truly converted cannot be content just living with an unbelieving husband. If the Lord means anything to her, she will want to do everything in her power to lead him to Christ. The apostle Peter outlines the procedure.

> Wives, likewise, be submissive to your own husbands, that even if some do not obey the word, they, without a word, may be won by the conduct of their wives, when they observe your chaste conduct accompanied by fear. Do not let your adornment be merely outward—arranging the hair, wearing gold, or putting on fine apparel—rather let it be the hidden person of the heart, with the incorruptible beauty of a gentle and quiet spirit, which is very precious in the sight of God (1 Peter 3:1–4).

- When making yeast bread, the recipe calls for mixing the ingredients, kneading the dough, and setting it aside to rise.

  What occurs in a few hours?

  What ingredient caused this result?

  How noisy was the dough?

- Compare this bread-making process to the Word at work in a woman's life so that her husband may be won "without a word."

The husband of a believing wife should see what three things in her conduct? (1) ________________ (2) ____________________ (3) ______________ and ____________ spirit.

## WHAT *NOT* TO DO

Before looking at the positive side of the instructions, notice some implied don'ts.

1. *She should not leave him.* Peter concurs with Paul's advice. She is to remain with her husband as long as he does not send her away. Remember that women were hardly more than chattel before Christ came. Husbands, especially heathen husbands, treated their wives as their possessions and did with them as they saw fit. Such a husband did not value the sanctity of marriage. If he refused to live with her, there was nothing she could do about it.

2. *She should not argue or nag.* The entire tenor of the passage implies a living example of the effect of Christianity upon a person's life.

## WHAT TO DO

Peter does not give mere suggestions. Rather, he gives divine commands regarding a wife's conduct toward her unbelieving husband.

1. *She is to be in subjection to her husband.* Of course God's commands have to be first in her life, and she must obey God rather than her husband when there is a conflict. But in other matters she is to obey her husband. (See chapter 1 regarding a wife's submission.)

2. *She is to win her husband by her conduct.* Only one thing can convert a person: the Word of God. "So then faith comes by hearing, and hearing by the word of God" (Romans 10:17). First Peter 3:1 tells what the wife may do if her husband does not obey the word. In the

original language "the" is included in this phrase. "The word" can mean only the Word of God. A person must learn the truth before he can accept it. When a husband hears and still will not obey, the only thing a wife can do is teach him by her example.

First Peter 3:1 says literally: "They, without a word, may be won by the conduct of their wives." "The" does not appear before "word" in the original language. So the second time "word" is used in this passage, it refers to a word from the wife and not the Word of God. Instead of nagging him about his failure to obey the gospel, the wife may win him by her conduct—manner of life.

*Wives, likewise, be submissive to your own husbands, that even if some do not obey ______ word, they, without ____ word, may be won by the ______________ of their wives, when they observe your ____________ conduct accompanied by fear. Do not let your adornment be merely outward—arranging the hair, wearing gold, or putting on fine apparel—rather let it be the hidden person of the ____________, with the incorruptible beauty of a gentle and quiet ____________, which is very precious in the sight of God* (1 Peter 3:1–4).

An unbelieving husband should see the following traits in his wife:

1. *Pure conduct.* Proper comportment demonstrates the presence of Christ through his Word within her. Her life truly becomes a living sacrifice (Romans 12:1). Her daily life demonstrates each principle of Christianity.

2. *Reverence.* Husbands "may be won by the conduct of their wives, when they observe your chaste conduct accompanied by fear [reverence]" (1 Peter 3:1–2).

3. *A meek and quiet spirit.* Because of the depth of her inward beauty, the Christian woman does not have to resort to gaudy clothes in order to attract attention.

## EVERY MOVE WILL BE WATCHED

Every Christian woman should strive to be as Christlike as possible. A Christian husband is not as likely to scrutinize his wife's behavior as much as an unbelieving husband does. A believing husband realizes how difficult it is to live godly each day and will be more sympathetic toward his wife's weaknesses. In fact, a godly husband can be a great source of strength to help you through trying times. An unbelieving husband, on the other hand, is likely to watch every move you make so he can bring criticism to your faith.

One husband told how he watched his Christian wife for years before he obeyed the gospel. He deliberately tried to throw obstacles in her path that would have kept the ordinary Christian from worship and Bible study—any church activity—just to see how she would handle them. During all those trying years when the children were small, she faithfully attended all services. He tried to take the children to a denomination with him, but she refused to allow that. Now he is a genuinely dedicated Christian. "If she had given in to me," he said, "I would never have been receptive to the truth."

> "If she had given in to me, I'd never have been receptive to the truth."

*Be steadfast,* ________________, *always* ________________ *in the work of the Lord, knowing that your labor is not in* ____________ *in the Lord* (1 Corinthians 15:58).

Your husband may know more than you realize what is expected of you in your Christian life. When he sees that you do not worship faithfully (Hebrews 10:25)—you offer flimsy excuses—he rightfully concludes that your religion is not very important to you. (Don't attend services with a martyr complex. He must see a real joy in your attendance.) He hears the preacher say that Christians are soul winners. When you make no attempt to teach the unsaved, your husband probably decides you do not truly think unbelievers will be lost.

How many good works does he see in your life? He knows a Christian should give aid to the downtrodden, the sick, the bereaved. When did he last see you prepare a dish for someone in need? And what about your temperament? He may not be able to quote Galatians 5:22–23, but he knows that a Christian should have a better disposition than someone who does not profess to have the fruit of the Spirit. Does he see love, joy, peace, longsuffering, gentleness, goodness, faith, meekness, and temperance in your life? Or does he live with a shrew?

*Be ______________ to present yourself approved to God, a ______________ who does not need to be ashamed, ______________ dividing the word of truth* (2 Timothy 2:15).

Your spouse may not know the exact words of 2 Timothy 2:15, but he has enough sense to conclude that a Christian should study the Bible regularly. Do you have a time set aside for daily meditation upon God's Word? No spiritual activity should be done in a manner that calls attention to good works, but does your husband ever see you with a Bible in hand?

Peter tells Christian women to win their husbands by their conduct. This broad category—translated "conversation" in the King James Version—certainly covers the use of the tongue.

So what about your conduct? Does your tongue speak kind words, or is it so caustic that it drives him further from the truth? You should never nag in an attempt to get him to obey God. Guard every statement you make concerning the Lord's church. If you constantly criticize the church leaders and programs of the church, don't be surprised when your husband concludes that you worship with a rotten group of hypocrites. Do you really blame him for not wanting to be a part of such a group? Is the church the most important thing in your life? Or do you spend more time in clubs and civic activities than you do in the work of the church?

Here is a summary of Peter's admonitions to the wife of an unbeliever: *You should be the best wife you can be, in every respect.* That includes the kindness and consideration you show your husband, the way you manage your house, and the manner in which you treat his relatives. Christianity should permeate every phase of your life.

The unbelieving husband will be observing his Christian wife in all areas of conduct. Comment on her behavior in the following categories:

Faithful attendance at services:

Soul winning:

Good works:

Temperament:

Bible study:

Use of the tongue:

Putting God first:

## PROBLEMS TO BE SOLVED

Be a good wife by showing kindness and consideration. A Christian woman cannot compromise her convictions in her long-range efforts to win him to Christ. She must always put God first. The following passages emphasize this principle:

- Matthew 10:37—"He who loves father or mother more than Me is not worthy of Me. And he who loves son or daughter more than Me is not worthy of Me."
- Mark 10:29–30—"Assuredly, I say to you, there is no one who has left house or brothers or sisters or father or mother or wife or children or lands, for My sake and the gospel's, who shall not receive a hundredfold now in this time—houses and brothers and sisters and mothers and children and lands, with persecutions—and in the age to come, eternal life."
- Matthew 6:33—"But seek first the kingdom of God and His righteousness, and all these things shall be added to you."

Your husband may test your convictions, but he will respect you for them if you are really sincere and consistent.

- *Missing services*—Some women, in an effort to get their husbands to attend worship with them, will compromise by staying home with him part of the time. For example, the wife may miss ten o'clock Bible study just to get her husband to the eleven o'clock worship hour. Or she may stay at home on Wednesday night if he will attend all the services on Sunday. Your lips may not say it, but actions are telling your husband that you think Hebrews 10:25 is a lie.
- *Attending denominational services*—Many unbelieving husbands have no religious convictions. Some, however, are very faithful in

attending their denominations. Some wives feel justified in attending with their husbands one week if they will attend with them the next week. Those women fail to realize that they are supporting, by their presence, something they believe to be contrary to God's Word. Remember, you are married to Christ.

- *Contribution*—A Christian woman with a non-Christian husband often has a special problem giving to God from the family treasury. She wants to give as they have been prospered, but her husband is not always so quick to make a contribution to something that has no meaning to him. Her giving will be dependent upon how much freedom she is given in managing the family income. Except in rare cases, most women have some part of the family income to cover household expenses. By practicing wise management and thrift, surely a wife can save some part of that amount to give to God.

- *Worship while on vacation*—A Christian couple can plan their vacation so they can be near a congregation of the Lord for worship. If they must be in an area where Christians are not meeting, they can prepare their worship without others. The wife of an unbeliever cannot so easily do that, so if a woman is to be faithful to God, she must have a clear understanding with her husband before the trip begins. If he plans to be in an area where there are no other Christians and she knows she will not be able to worship, can she justifiably make such a trip for pleasure?

Remember, you are married to Christ.

Problems will also arise concerning going out of town on Sundays to visit relatives or to sightsee. The husband may feel that since he works all week he is entitled to a day with his family. He should not have to be bothered with worship. Again, a Christian woman must remain firm in her convictions.

- *Children attending denominational services*—Many women with non-Christian husbands face the problem of allowing the children to attend church with their husbands. He will claim that the children are half his and he has the right to take them with him half the time. Logically, that is true, but a Christian cannot allow her children to be taught something she knows to be wrong. Her convictions will receive a great testing in this area.

Why might a Christian woman believe that having an unbelieving husband provides her with an excuse for not taking Matthew 7:21 seriously? Summarize the verse and write your answer.

Prepare a questionnaire for the women who have been successful in leading their husbands to Christ. Ask for methods which were successful for them. Discuss in class.

## Conclusion

Some women obey the gospel after marriage. Those whose husbands object have a difficult lot in life, but they are to be admired for doing what they know is right in spite of adversity. Others are Christians before they marry. They know that an ideal marriage can only be between members of the Lord's body. If only more older women who have experienced living with a non-Christian husband would share with them the heartache involved, there might be fewer mixed marriages. Every young bride thinks her case will be different. She feels that she will be successful in leading her husband to Christ, but the odds are against her. In a survey made among Christians, of every forty-nine who marry unbelievers, only twenty-one remain faithful. Of those, only nine are successful in converting their partners. Not everyone is receptive to the gospel. The parable of the sower teaches that only a portion of the seed will fall onto good ground (Matthew 13:1–9).

Every young bride thinks her case will be different.

A woman who marries outside the church is taking a very big risk. Not only might she be unable to convert her husband, but she may also lose her own soul. Her only course of action, if her husband will not obey the preaching of the Word, is to translate that Word into her daily living. She may live a sermon before him. If he is honest and receptive to the truth, that living sermon will bring forth fruit.

THE FOLLOWING WELL-KNOWN BOOKS FEATURE JANE MCWHORTER'S WRITING:

*Caterpillars or Butterflies*

*Let This Cup Pass*

*Meet My Friend David*

*My Sister's Keeper*

*Living Together in Knowledge*

*Friendship, Handle with Care*

*We Bow Down*

*Special Delivery*

*Roses in December*

*Now I Can Fly*

Brenda Taylor- 479-250-2722

Jessica